KA

ŽIŽKOV

Olšany Cemetery

VINOHRADY

VRŠOVICE

A KINGDOM OF SOULS

PRAGUE
CITY OF TORMENT

*

A KINGDOM
OF SOULS

by

DANIELA HODROVÁ

translated from the Czech by
VÉRONIQUE FIRKUSNY
&
ELENA SOKOL

JANTAR PUBLISHING 2015

First published in London, Great Britain in 2015 by
Jantar Publishing Ltd
www.jantarpublishing.com

Czech edition first published in Ústí nad Labem in 1991 as
Podobojí

Daniela Hodrová
A Kingdom of Souls
All rights reserved

A CIP catalogue record for this book is available from the British Library.
ISBN 978-0-9568890-5-8

Printed and bound in the Czech Republic by EUROPRINT a.s.

This translation was made possible by a grant from the Ministry of Culture of the Czech Republic.

MINISTRY OF CULTURE
CZECH REPUBLIC

CONTENTS

INTRODUCTION

The city is part of me and I am part of it, we are one being.

DANIELA HODROVÁ[*]

In late 1977, when Daniela Hodrová (born 1946) began writing her first novel, *A Kingdom of Souls* (*Podobojí* in the original Czech), the mood in Prague, the city of her birth, was bleak. By then, nearly a decade had passed since the 'Prague Spring' had been suppressed by the Soviet-led Warsaw-Pact invasion of Czechoslovakia on 21 August 1968. A year later, the Czechoslovak army's tanks rolled into Prague to quash the civic demonstration planned for the first anniversary of the invasion. In January 1969, a university student, Jan Palach, had immolated himself in protest against the people's apparent acceptance of the growing 'normalization' that represented a return to pre-reform hard-line communism. It would be almost two decades before a hint of Gorbachev's *glasnost* reforms reached Czechoslovakia. Yet even then, in the late 1980s, Czechs could not have anticipated the Velvet Revolution of November 1989, which led to the downfall of the Czechoslovak Communist regime and soon brought an exhilarating sense of renewal to their land.

Unlike that of many of her fellow Czech writers, Hodrová's

---

[*] Daniela Dražanová, 'An Interview with Daniela Hodrová,' *The Prague Review* 2 (Winter 1966), p. 104.

iii

early prose did not appear in unofficial *samizdat* editions, nor was it published abroad in the exile press. However, *Podobojí* did circulate among a broad group of friends and colleagues as an anonymous manuscript, and finally was brought out by a provincial publisher in 1991. It was followed, in quick succession, by her second and third novels, *Kukly* (Puppets, 1991) and *Théta* (1992), both published in Prague. A second edition of those three works appeared in one volume, as a loose trilogy, *Trýznivé město* (City of Torment, 1992), an allusion to *città dolente* from Dante's *Inferno*.

After completing secondary school in 1963, Hodrová had originally hoped to devote herself to the theatre, even to become an actress. She had spent many magical hours in her childhood behind the scenes of the well-known Vinohrady Theatre, watching her actor father, Zdeněk Hodr, perform. However, after a year as a director's assistant and script consultant at a small Prague theatre, she chose instead to pursue another of her serious interests — literature. While theatre would remain one of her passions, as well as an important motif in her prose, it is the city of Prague — its *genius loci* — that lies at the heart of all her fiction. Indeed, it was Hodrová's own childhood room of her family's fifth floor flat on Vinohradská Street, with its window overlooking the Olšany Cemetery across the way, that inspired the opening sentence of *A Kingdom of Souls*, from which all her subsequent prose has emanated. The character Alice Davidovič has a prototype in the young Jewish girl who jumped from that very window to avoid being transported to a Nazi concentration camp (a historical fact the author learned only when she was older).

Having discovered her love of writing as a child, Hodrová would pursue a dual career as a prose writer and literary theorist, not unlike Umberto Eco. Even before she finished her studies of Czech and Russian literature at Charles University (1969), she had already published her earliest scholarly essays during the liberal days of 1968. She went on to post-graduate studies in French and comparative literature, and in the early 1970s worked for three years as an editor for the Odeon Publishing House. Finally, in 1975,

Hodrová was accepted as a research scholar in the Department of Literary Theory at what today is known as the Academy of Sciences Institute of Czech Literature. (The Academy awarded her the highest post-doctoral degree in 1992.) During a long career at the Institute, she has been immensely productive in her area of specialization — the theory of the novel. Her first published book, *Hledání románu* (In Search of the Novel, 1989), treats the typological opposition between the novel as reality and as fiction, reminding us of her own creative experiments in that genre. Her pioneering study of the novel of initiation, *Román zasvěcení*, first appeared in 1993 (revised and expanded edition, 2014). Ever sensitive to the world around her, in the last decade she has gone on to explore themes in more broadly conceived cultural studies, with aspects of the city still a central focus. Recently, Hodrová has received well-deserved recognition for her lifetime of writing: she was awarded the prestigious Czech State Prize for Literature in 2011, followed by the distinguished international Franz Kafka Prize in 2012.

Situating Hodrová in a broader literary context, critics often categorize her prose as postmodern and typically draw comparisons with such contemporary Czech male writers as Michal Ajvaz (b. 1949) and Jiří Kratochvil (b. 1940). However, there are other important literary affinities to keep in mind, such as the rich matrilineal tradition of Czech 'experimental' writing represented by Milada Součková (1899–1983) and Věra Linhartová (b. 1938), as well as the intriguing non-traditional narratives of Hodrová's contemporaries Sylvie Richterová (b. 1945), Alexandra Berková (1949–2003), and Zuzana Brabcová (b. 1959).

In an essay Hodrová contributed to a volume on the contemporary European novel, her characterization of the breakdown of linearity in 20th-century European writing, especially writing by women, captures well the essence of her own style:

> The rigid structure of the novel, traditionally divided into chapters, collapses; the text is often composed of a sequence

of loosely connected paragraphs, riddled with ellipses. This fragmentation corresponds to a descent into the past, fore-grounding the text and recording the fleeting present. ...The narrative in these cases is frequently conceived as a search for narrative and story....[*]

(In this connection she mentions the French writers Nathalie Sarraute, Marguerite Duras, and Sylvie Germain; and one could also include Virginia Woolf.)[†] In her extensive study of modern narrative *Citlivé město* (The Sensible City, 2006), Hodrová has articulated an understanding of the fundamentally gendered nature of contemporary prose, including her own, using familiar concepts from ancient Chinese philosophy, yin and yang (female and male principles) to characterize two basic types of texts: 'woven texts' (yin texts), in contrast to 'flowing texts' (yang texts).[‡] While a text as flowing has a tendency towards a single perspective, a text as weaving embodies multiple perspectives. The woven text has the character of 'a net or tissue' in which there are many centres or knots, with no overt beginning or ending; it embodies both a broader collective consciousness, and also the unconscious, re-plete with collective, archetypal, and mythological-metaphorical associations.[§] It is no surprise that Carl Gustav Jung is one of Hodrová's favourite thinkers.

In all of Hodrová's prose there is a rich interpenetration of past

---

[*] D. Hodrová, 'Woven into the Web,' trans. A. Zucker, in U. Keller, I. Rakusa (eds), *Writing in Europe*, Budapest: ECU Press, 2004, p. 147.

[†] See E. Sokol, 'A City of one's own: the intersection of urban space and consciousness in novels by Daniela Hodrová and Virginia Woolf,' *Slovo a smysl. Word & Sense* 15, 8 (2011), pp. 40–56.

[‡] See E. Sokol, 'Spinning her Web: Novels of Daniela Hodrová through a Gendered Lens,' in R. Marsh (ed.), *New Women's Writing in Russia, Central and Eastern Europe: Gender, Generation and Identities*, Newcastle upon Tyne: Cambridge Scholars Publishing, 2012, pp. 280–297.

[§] D. Hodrová, *Citlivé město (eseje z mytopoetiky)*, Prague: Akropolis, 2006, pp. 80, 100, 109.

and present, reminiscent of Marcel Proust's style in his fictional epic *In Search of Lost Time*. Time for her becomes a spatial rather than a linear dimension. Thus, the intermingling of the living and the dead is a central feature of her prose, beginning with this first novel. Readers intrigued by the magical realism of such writers as Gabriel Garcia Marquez will appreciate Hodrová's own endeavours in that tradition. (*One Hundred Years of Solitude* first appeared in Czech translation in 1971.)

Multiple meanings, so characteristic of Hodrová's prose, are already at play in the original Czech title of her first novel. The Czech word *podobojí* literally means 'in both kinds', referring to the Eucharist. Most concretely it refers to communion with both bread and wine, which in the context of Czech history was a symbol of a pre-Reformation compromise with Church practices gained after the death of Jan Hus in 1415.[*] By way of allusion it is also linked to the St Bartholomew's Day Massacre of the French Huguenots in Paris in 1572. As the reader will quickly sense, duality, doubling in general, is a repeated theme in this novel.

For those not familiar with Czech history, some details of significant historical and cultural allusions in *A Kingdom of Souls* may prove helpful. On one level, it is a loose historical allegory, most of the narrative takes place from the time of World War II through to the 1970s; years that include the Nazi occupation, the uprising in Prague during the last days of the war and ensuing forced resettlement of the Germans, the communist coup of February 1948, and, of course, the hope-filled Prague Spring, followed by the Warsaw-Pact invasion and the subsequent period of oppressive political normalization. Mythology and earlier

---

[*] 'Protestantism' in the Czech sense, may be thought to have begun one hundred years before Martin Luther's 'Ninety-Five Theses' of 1517. Prague had its own reformer, Jan Hus, who along with others, campaigned against the excesses of the church and for a change in Liturgy. Hus was burned as a heretic in Konstanz, Germany in 1415. His followers became known as the Hussites and eventually settled for what became the special Bohemian liturgy known as 'Eucharist in both kinds' or *podobojí* in Czech.

eras of Czech history play their roles too. There are allusions to Blaník Mountain, where legendary knights led by St Wenceslas are said to be sleeping, destined to awaken to defend the Czech nation in its time of greatest trouble; and also to the figure of the mythical White Lady. We return to important historical periods, including the early Czech 15th-century church reforms led by Jan Hus (1368–1415) with its wars, the Reformation inspired by Luther, then the Counter-Reformation and Habsburg domination after the defeat of the Protestants at the Battle of White Mountain in 1620, the 19th-century National Revival, some of whose participants are buried at the Olšany Cemetery, and finally the First Czechoslovak Republic, a democratic state that lasted only twenty years (1918–1938). Most of the novel's action takes place in Vinohrady, the region of Prague that lies south-east of the historical centre and where Charles IV laid out the royal vineyards in the mid-14th century. That district also served as a burial ground for plague victims in the middle ages. The frequently mentioned Bartholomew Street, located in the Old Town, held the headquarters of the notorious secret police during the communist regime (a police station still stands there today). The 'fiery furnace', of course, evokes Jan Palach's tragic act in front of the National Museum, across the street from Dům potravin (the Food Bazaar in this translation).

Through playful poetic prose, imaginatively blending historical and cultural motifs with autobiographical moments, Daniela Hodrová shares her unique perception of Prague. *A Kingdom of Souls* is the first volume of this author's literary journey — an unusual quest for self, for one's place in life and in the world, a world that for Hodrová is embodied in Prague. Since she first depicted Alice Davidovič's fateful journey through her bedroom window, followed by the subsequent rich narrative of *A Kingdom of Souls*, Hodrová has written nine more intriguing volumes of prose, each new work in some sense a continuation of the previous ones, and all set largely in Prague. In interviews, Hodrová has confessed that she is writing one big Novel that will end only with her death.

Highly self-conscious and at times even self-referential, each of her narratives is a complex network of fictional and real characters, along with spatial and temporal interrelationships, all woven into a rich texture of literary, mythological, and historical allusions — sophisticated texts that make serious demands on us as readers. Yet, as the author insists, they were written intuitively — perhaps for that reason they have the power magically to captivate us, too.

Elena Sokol
Wooster, Ohio
August 2014

PRONUNCIATION GUIDE

CZECH	ENGLISH EQUIVALENT
á	as in *father*
	e.g. Zásmuky, Kollár, Vinohradská
c	as in *hits*
	e.g. Cyrila
č	as in *cheese*
	e.g. Davidovič, Klečka, Botič, Havlíček
ch	as in *Bach*
	e.g. Och
ě	as in *yes*
	e.g. Budějovice, Vojtěch
í	as in *neat*
	e.g. Blaník, Bubeník
j	as in *yoyo*
	e.g. Vojtěch, Budějovice
ou	as in *owe*
	e.g. Houba, Koudelka
ř	approximately as in *bourgeois*
	e.g. Mařenka, Přemysl (cf. Dvořák)
š	as in *sheep*
	e.g. Olšany, Diviš, Soška, Šafařík, Bartošek
ž	as in *measure*
	e.g. Žižkov

Alice Davidovič would never have thought the window of her childhood room hung so low over the Olšany Cemetery that a body could travel the distance in less than two seconds.

A sound in the pantry, as if someone was softly moaning. Alice enters and sees her grandmother at the table, tears streaming down her cheeks. The table is spread with the Sabbath tablecloth. It occurs to Alice that maybe one day someone will have a dress made of it, a Sabbath dress.

— Grandmother, why are you crying? asks Alice, and Grandmother Davidovič points to the corner: Can't you see, Grandfather is peeling onions. — But Grandfather is... — Shhh, Grandmother Davidovič puts a finger to her lips. Grandfather Davidovič, peeling onions in the corner, as if having heard Alice's objection in full, gives a wry laugh. Alice realizes her mistake, although until the moment she entered the pantry, she knew for certain that Grandfather had died three months ago, she could distinctly remember the day he returned from Mrs Soška's, where he'd been staying for many years. Grandfather had come back to the pantry to die, his whole body mangled by the Germans who had racked him and broken him on the wheel at Hagibor. And then he couldn't move any more and Grandmother tended him like a little child. Every morning, as she dressed him, Grandfather threatened to go back to Mrs Soška, but then he always grew silent and stayed seated where Grandmother had put him until evening, just giving a wry laugh every now and then, laughing even as she undressed him and put him to bed later on. As if with

1

that laughter Grandfather Davidovič was trying to say: It won't do you any good anyway, I'll go to Mrs Soška's again, I'll go just to spite you. But he didn't go anywhere because he felt ashamed before Mrs Soška, appearing so pitiful — and besides, he could have got there only by crawling on all fours.

Alice didn't know how to cover up her words and so she asked Grandmother Davidovič why she had put out the Sabbath tablecloth that day. And Grandmother was greatly surprised: Have you forgotten, dearie, that today Pavel Santner is coming to ask Grandfather for your hand? He's the one who brought the onions when he stopped by this morning. He was happy to hear you're feeling a little better.

Alice Davidovič didn't know where Grandmother got such ideas, the ones about Pavel Santner and the onions. Pavel Santner was indeed her beau but had left with a transport two weeks before. And even if, perhaps, he were here, he was unlikely to bring them onions. And why would he come to ask Grandfather for her hand when Grandfather was, after all … Besides, Alice wasn't sure Pavel Santner wanted to marry her, he wasn't the type to think about marriage, he wasn't even thinking about it as he held Alice in his arms before his departure, it was she who had wished it, not he, because his mind was already entirely somewhere else. And later on, as Alice watched him walking away along the Olšany Cemetery, watched him from the window of her childhood room, from the window of her eighteen-year-old room, he never even raised his eyes towards her.

In the pantry, Grandmother Davidovič again began to wail softly, maybe it wasn't really weeping, maybe it was a Sabbath prayer. Alice Davidovič closed the door carefully behind her. She was trying to decide whether to put on her best dress or be naked when Pavel Santner arrived. He must have come back since he brought onions for Grandmother Davidovič, he's probably sure to come since Grandmother Davidovič has put out the Sabbath tablecloth and Grandfather Davidovič has risen from the dead. In all likelihood, he really will come to ask for her hand, even though it is all very strange.

In the end she decided on the dress, its white collar had wrinkled a little from hanging in the wardrobe so long because it was wartime and Alice had stopped going to the theatre, but there was no time to touch it up with an iron, Pavel Santner could be here any minute. She felt a bit shy now, after what had happened between them the last time, she didn't even know if it had given him pleasure, if he liked her at all, she was not really pretty, and once she grew old she would be as ugly as Grandmother Davidovič. Pavel Santner most likely knew that and therefore might not come at all to ask Grandfather Davidovič for her hand, most likely he had changed his mind, telling himself Alice Davidovič was worth just the onions, and perhaps not even those, perhaps not even those.

By now it is dark and the path along the Olšany Cemetery remains deserted, no one is coming. And Grandmother Davidovič in the pantry has grown quiet, she may have laid her head on the Sabbath tablecloth and fallen asleep because she found the waiting too long. And were Alice to enter now, Grandfather Davidovič would no longer be there. — Don't say he left through the lightwell, Grandmother. And there would be no trace of onions either because they haven't had onions in a long time, it's just that Grandmother Davidovič had been talking about them yesterday, how she would love to make onion soup, that soup would certainly do Alice good, if only she had at least one onion, at least one.

Frau Hergesell had a dress made from the tablecloth. After all, Frau Hergesell didn't know it was a Sabbath tablecloth and that Grandmother Davidovič had laid it on the table the day Alice Davidovič after a long time once again put on her best dress and flew from the window of her childhood room to meet Pavel Santner. Frau Hergesell knew only that a Jewish family had lived in the flat before them and that someone from the family had jumped out of a window the day before they were to join a transport. Frau Hergesell would have forgotten about this long ago were it not for the onion odour she could always smell there, in vain did she keep trying to air out the rooms. She complained frequently to Herr Hergesell, a court clerk, as they lay next to each other in the room whose windows overlooked the Olšany Cemetery. — It's still here, that onion smell. Each time, Herr Hergesell explained to her that the smell was retained by the furniture and the walls. — Did they eat nothing but onions?

After the war, in Jena, when Frau Hergesell reminisced about the Prague years, the obtrusive onion odour kept coming back. She had carried it with her already at the time of her hasty departure from Prague. She could even smell it on the shoulder of her older son Rudi, as she leaned her head there. Even her son smelled of Jewish onions, just like the furniture, even her son.

THE PANTRY

I am the pantry, the chamber of resurrection. My one window — my one little window — is blind and doesn't open onto this world. When it's ajar, centuries-old dust falls in, dust from the dreams and lives of others, it covers the cracked paint of the table upon which Grandmother Davidovič rested her head. And after her the maid Cyrila rested her head upon that table, and after her the hunchbacked maid Anežka, and after her the maid Mařenka from the village of Karhule near Blaník Mountain... Suffer little children to come unto me. I am the chamber of ravishers preying on country ninnies, I am the chamber of shivering small-time thieves and masturbating youths, I am the chamber of suicides, and the chamber of dreamers. I belong to all those who enter and soil me with their secret sins, with their petty vices. I take them all indiscriminately into my decrepit arms, press them to my hermaphrodite body, for I have lost all female charms in my old age, my source of femininity dried up long ago. I am a wasteland. My element is the lightwell dust settling in my entrails until the time of the next folding of the earth. I am what my visitors make

4

of me, they come to gratify me as they would an aged harlot, only in moments of hopelessness and anxiety. I am the memory of dreams piling up in the dust at my feet and turning into dust, and of other dreams arising from dust. And the bird asleep upside down, near the ceiling, wakes up at such times and flies about flapping its wings against the walls, against the lightwell window, against the child's face shining in the half-light. And at other times it changes into a mouse, or rather into a rat.

Is it a rat, the Chambermaid, or a bird, the Chamberlain, bowing subserviently to Vojtěch and Diviš, the tails of its frock coat blowing in the draft? It is a bird-rat. And when children secretly enter the pantry bringing leftovers from their snack, they never know whether they'll find the rat or the bird there. Or is it always both? The ambiguous spirit of the pantry, the bird-rat born from the mixture of dust, rags, fur from old coats, scraps of paper, and a life-giving word. And there was a bird-rat. It was certainly necessary for all these components to combine under singular, unrepeatable circumstances, perhaps on a day when a ray of sunlight reached in through the lightwell (there were few such days in a year, if any at all) — for a fraction of time long enough to accomplish the miracle of bringing matter to life. The spirit of the pantry came into the world in the likeness of a rat and a bird, at least that was how it appeared to the children's imagination. It lived and grew fat, for the hand of the little children was generous. It is naïve to suppose that such an ambiguous creature lives only on dust because it was born of dust. It wants its daily ration, it demands its bread — the doughy centre for the Chamberlain, the crust for the Chambermaid. It nuzzles up to those who feed it, to their feet and cheeks, brushing against them with the tails of its frock coat, it squeaks and rustles. Or is that a soft breeze making its way through the crack under the window? For when the maid Cyrila, or Jan Paskal, or his wife Nora Paskal, enters, the spirit instantly vanishes, it hides in the lightwell and waits, waits until the coast is clear.

From the children's talk the maid Cyrila gathers there is a

mouse in the pantry and sets a trap for the night. Cyrila, however, does not know that, be it a bird or a rat, the Chamberlain or the Chambermaid, it will only eat from a child's hand. And so the next day Cyrila finds nothing but a dust ball in the trap, unless, in fact, it was a small feather or a few hairs plucked from the servile little animal with a dual nature. And if the children had any notion of reincarnation, they would have to conclude that the spirit of both Grandfather Davidovič and Grandmother Davidovič dwells in the pantry. When it picks the bread from their hand, the spirit loses itself in melancholy reminiscences and melancholy dreams. And when it is alone again in the pantry, it turns back into a tattered rag or a dust ball wafted in through the lightwell of time.

THE ST BARTHOLOMEW'S DAY MASSACRE

Blaise Pascal? — By no means: Jan Paskal, pastor Paskal, an inconsequential brother of the Bohemian Brethren. Evidently he has nothing in common with the great Frenchman whose mind stretched across two abysses and who wrote the *Treatise on Vacuum*, nothing except, perhaps, his Lutheranism, as Mistress Nora would refer to his faith later on. Pastor Paskal believes himself a descendant of an old Huguenot family who had been forced to leave France after the St Bartholomew's Day Massacre. But why won't he admit when he first began to believe that? In the days when Jan Paskal used to browse through the parish records, he discovered a whole lot of Paskals and Paschals in the Krkonoše Mountain region, ones who, however, had probably forgotten that day of horrors, having spent all their lives at the loom. A street in a little town actually bears the name of one of them, Jan Paskal later calls it an alley, a diagonal one, known as Paschal Lane, supposedly it leads to the cemetery, weaving among the little houses as if it had drunk one too many. It is named after a cleric, also of the Bohemian Brethren, but this one His Reverence Jan Paskal is willing to acknowledge as family, this one yes, while he won't talk much about the rural weavers since that would be grist for Mistress Nora's mill. For she hasn't believed the Pascal legend for some time, and maintains that Paskal is probably a common Czech name changed by someone who didn't want to be called Pusskill or Puscall. Be that as it may, the name was well suited to Jan Paskal's vocation, the pastor was happy with it. That happiness was marred only by the thought of the maid Cyrila who liked to mispronounce it, may the Lord forgive her, she didn't stay with the Paskals long, growing gradually weaker and weaker, until finally she faded away to a mere threadbare tatter, a little tuft of wispy cloth, and even that disappeared somewhere in the pantry, even that.

For Jan Paskal, the pantry was his St Bartholomew's Day Massacre. It was the St Bartholomew's chamber where two Catholics would flay his Protestant skin. And the moment when he felt his body taut between the two royal flayers, between the two flayers of the St Bartholomew's Day Massacre, between Mr Sanglier and Mr Mortier (the first French names the image brought to his mind), the Count Jean de Pascal (it never hurts to be of noble birth) fancied himself to be just like the famous Blaise Pascal of Port-Royal, stretched between his two voids.

What more went on to happen in the St Bartholomew's chamber is obscured by its centuries-old darkness allowing only a glimpse of Count Jean de Pascal, who by some miracle had saved his skin and thereafter absconded with it far away from the royally set table and the bloody banquet, to hide somewhere near the mountains in a God-forsaken hamlet in Bohemia, and there to bring forth descendants born of a dairymaid, descendants without titles, spinning their lives like silkworms.

THE SCENT OF KAIN

Pastor Jan Paskal denies his parents. They don't suit his Protestant legend. Jan Paskal cannot very well explain how it came about

7

that weavers from the foothills of the Krkonoše Mountains in the north happened to end up in the southern town of Budějovice. He suspects a rebellion somewhere in the past, the escape of a silkworm who grew weary of spinning from dawn to dusk. Jakub Paskal runs away from home and learns the tailor's trade. But one Markéta from a travelling theatre company subsequently turns his head and takes him along on the road through the Czech lands. Silkworm Paskal plays King Lear and produces a son christened Jan. Then comes the first world war, the company falls apart. The parents settle in Budějovice, in a garret. Jakub Paskal resumes his trade.

When it rains, the roof above little Jan Paskal's head rings like angel chimes. And behind a partition there is Kain. Jan is sure Kain is their tenant. He has never seen him, but every now and then he hears his father or mother talking to him. — Say, Kain, how do you like your new coat? Jan Paskal thinks Kain is his father's journeyman. He lives in the adjoining alcove where old theatre costumes and coats hang, awaiting Mr Paskal's alterations. Kain must have been an actor too, because when Master Paskal goes away in search of provisions, Mistress Markéta comes to Kain to reminisce about the old days. She also comes to ponder the words of a prophecy — The Mountain will take you away, the Mountain. So far they make no sense, like the mention of the wood in Macbeth. They were pronounced by Billy the Goat, the organ-grinder, in a Budějovice courtyard.

Every time Mistress Markéta comes back from visiting Kain, a strange scent wafts through the air to Jan. Kain's dwelling must be utterly permeated with it. During the day, Jan hears his father telling stories to Kain as he sews, but Kain always remains silent. He must be mute, thinks Jan, he is mute like Billy the Goat who cranks the barrel-organ in their courtyard and tells fortunes for a bowl of soup. He does so only when Master Paskal is not at home, because Master Paskal doesn't like his sort of goatish heresies. But Billy the Goat at least mumbles something, even though no one can understand a word, while Kain remains silent as a fish.

8

One day Jan Paskal is at home alone. The coats hanging all over the place, even over his little bed like a canopy, come alive. Their sleeves become animated and the coats begin to communicate with one another. Jan Paskal grows rather anxious. He knocks on the partition: Kain, are you there? No answer. Jan knocks harder and harder but all is silent behind the wall. Kain must be sleeping like a log. Or perhaps he has been forbidden to talk to Jan. The hollow sleeves of the coats reach out for Jan.

Jan gets up and goes to the adjoining alcove. Kain's scent wafts over him right by the door. At first he doesn't see anyone. He must push aside a whole pile of assorted costumes, including King Lear's. Behind them, all the way against the wall, which slants sharply under the roof, stands Kain. He is pretending to sleep but his eyes are open. And his hair, to Jan's surprise, is completely white and pulled back into a braid. — Kain! But Kain goes on pretending to sleep. It is then that Jan Paskal notices the coat Kain is wearing, the same one a marksman from Baron Fröhlich's regiment had brought to Master Paskal the day before to have its gold buttons resewn. So that's how it is, Jan Paskal thinks to himself. That's why he's pretending to sleep. Behind the partition, Kain furtively dresses up in other people's coats.

The next day little Judas Paskal tells on Kain. Master Paskal and Mistress Markéta are laughing, behind the partition Kain is probably laughing too, but quietly, so no one hears him. Ever since that day Jan Paskal hasn't liked Kain and fears Kain doesn't like him either, because he told on him, although Jan now knows that Kain is only a dressmaker's dummy, nothing more.

KAIN

I am Kain, wooden Kain, a dressmaker's dummy. I stand in an alcove, at the very top of the house, where the roof slants. When it rains, the roof above my head rings like angel chimes. A downpour in Budějovice sounds like drum rolls at the Last Judgment. At

9

such moments I am gripped by the fear that I may be mistaken for Cain who killed Abel.

— Say, Kain, how do you like your new coat? Master Paskal steps back to take a better look at the coat I have on. But no sooner done, someone, lord or vassal, comes in, takes off my coat and carries it away. Only Mistress Markéta, if she happens to be there, feels sorry for me: There they go, Kain, taking away your coat again. Master Paskal noticed my feelings for Mistress Markéta long ago, he jokes about my embarrassment at having to stand there before him in my wooden nakedness, wearing only the white braid on my head.

I am Kain, but in a moment I'm this one and then suddenly that one, today a judge, tomorrow a marksman, and the day after tomorrow maybe a priest, according to Master Paskal's whim. And I'm even a petty thief, slipping into other people's coats. That little Judas Paskal, he's the one who told on me. Right now I'm wearing the coat of a marksman from Baron Fröhlich's regiment, it suits me and Mistress Markéta really likes me in it. She steals in every other minute, stands at a distance, then comes closer, and sometimes even softly caresses me. — Why aren't you the marksman, Kain? She caresses me, yet doesn't feel my wooden heart pounding feverishly under the coat. Why aren't I a marksman?

And one afternoon the marksman himself comes in, it so happens that nobody is home apart from Mistress Markéta and me, Kain, except I seem to be invisible to them. The marksman tries to take the coat off me but I put up a fight, I don't want to stand here naked before Mistress Markéta, and I don't want to stand here like that before the marksman either. But she even helps him by undoing the buttons. And then the marksman doesn't fail to notice my ridiculous appearance without the coat, he even deliberately pushes the braid down over my eyes. And I can tell that Mistress Markéta doesn't much like his joke, she seems suddenly to grow a little sad, as if she were suddenly taken aback by something. But just then the marksman grasps her so, that she cries out in fright. And then the marksman begins to tell her something about having three houses in the town of Kutná Mountain and Mistress Markéta believes his every word. And that afternoon, Mistress Markéta goes off with the marksman to Kutná Mountain. And so the words of the goatish prophecy are fulfilled, so are they fulfilled.

THE MARK OF THE GOAT

According to the prediction made by Billy the Goat, the organ-grinder, in the Budějovice courtyard, the year 1914 marks the beginning of God's kingdom on earth, when Christ ascends the throne and wages his last battle with the Antichrist. According to the goatish prophecy, the end of the world is drawing near and only those marked on their foreheads as the chosen ones will be saved. Master Paskal doesn't believe in goatish heresies, he doesn't believe in them, not even since the day the Mountain indeed came and took Mistress Markéta away. — You didn't keep a good enough eye on her, Kain! Master Paskal yells down to the courtyard to ask whether Christ is there helping Billy the Goat crank his barrel organ, and sends Jan down with some soup. One bowl for Billy the Goat, another one for Christ. Master Paskal is generous, but Billy the Goat won't touch the other bowl.

Jan Paskal holds the bowl of soup and says to Billy the Goat: We've got a wooden Kain at home. Billy the Goat puts down his spoon and looks sternly at Jan: Cain killed Abel, so it is written. You worship idols, like the pagans. But Jan laughs because by now he knows that Kain in German means no one and that Father specifically gave him the name because Kain seems to exist while in fact he does not, or seems not to exist while in fact he does. Jan Paskal, however, doesn't like Kain, that's why he mentioned him to Billy the Goat. And Billy the Goat senses this, and every time Jan happens to be alone with him in the courtyard, he whispers in his ear: Kill Kain, the end of the world is near. Just take a good look at him, his forehead bears the mark of damnation.

Jan Paskal scrutinizes Kain. His naked eye discerns nothing, but as he touches Kain's forehead, he feels an elongated bulge, as if the wood had cracked there, and the forehead were coming apart in the middle. (Some years later he notices the same fissure on Nora Paskal's forehead and remembers the mark of the goat.)

The children are building a little fire in the courtyard, a St John's Eve bonfire. Or is it a heretic's stake? To make it burn better, seminarian Jan Paskal brings them Kain. Now he may do so, having buried his father, yes, now he may. The children put a newspaper hat on Kain's head, the kind that housepainters wear. — If you recant, Kain, we will pardon you. Oh, Kain, why don't you recant, you could be in the pantry now, talking to Grandfather and Grandmother Davidovič. Your presence would cheer them up. The flames are already licking Kain's legs. And when the flames reach Kain's forehead, seminarian Jan Paskal seems to see Kain's soul, a little white wisp, flutter from the crack. And the children shout: Gossamer! and chase the little wisp across the courtyard.

The flames consuming Kain on the Paskalian pyre are dying down, his peculiar scent rises from the fire, seeming to have become even more potent at the moment of death. The whole garret is filled with Kain's scent, it grasps seminarian Paskal, just as the Mountain grasped Mistress Markéta, it has been twelve years now since she was carried away. How naïve of Jan Paskal to think he can get rid of the scent this way. He doesn't realize that fire sets free the soul imprisoned in wood. The soul rises up to the window, Jan Paskal inhales it, he holds it in himself, he has breathed in Kain, he himself is now Kain, the damned one of the goatish prophecy, the one with the mark he feels on his own forehead.

BREAD AND COFFEE

Every Friday the seminarians from St Anna's go to the Institute for the Deaf-Mute in Marian Square. Every Friday they perform acts of charity there. Every Friday those who have attained a higher level preach God's word to the deaf-mute inmates. The others are still learning Christian humility, the others wash the feet of the deaf-mute inmates every Friday. Afterwards they all gather in the Institute's dining hall for their afternoon snack — white coffee and white bread. The white coffee and white bread are served by Anna Houba, an orphan, Anna Houba dances with the bread and coffee around the dining hall that reeks of the flour-thickened soup the deaf-mute inmates had for lunch. Anna Houba's smile sets the tonsures bowing down low over the table: *Averte, Domine, oculos meos...* Turn my eyes away from Anna Houba, oh Lord, they pray over their white coffee and their white bread. And as the seminarians eat their bread and sip their coffee, they feel as if they're receiving the body and blood of St Anna Houba.

The old organ-grinder Billy the Goat, soothsayer Goat, is living out the rest of his days in the Institute for the Deaf-Mute, but the source of his wisdom has dried up there, Billy the Goat no longer turns his crank nor does he foretell the future, his goatish kingdom has grown silent within him. When seminarian Jan Paskal washes his feet, he senses that Billy the Goat recognizes him. And Billy the Goat, as if angry at Jan about something, deliberately kicks his feet in the tin tub till the soapy water splashes into Paskal's eyes. For Billy the Goat knows that although Jan Paskal washes his feet every Friday, although Jan Paskal leaves him half his white bread and half his white coffee every Friday, he is still not humble or devout enough, his thoughts are not sufficiently pure. Billy the Goat knows that even now, as Jan Paskal washes his feet, he is thinking of Anna Houba, and he knows, too, that soon Jan will take her away, and the Institute for the Deaf-Mute will be orphaned.

And one day during an outing in the town of Budějovice, when the seminarians get away from their *pater spiritualis*, Jan Paskal hurries to where the Malše and Vltava rivers meet, where Anna Houba awaits him. He conceals his clerical collar with Anna's scarf, takes Anna Houba for a walk along the river and strolls with her on the Island, takes her up Piarist Street and along Canon Street, he even walks with her down Theatre Street. But Priest Street, the

13

street of his seminary, that one Jan Paskal avoids.

Anna Houba smells of coffee and bread, and Jan Paskal inhales that scent and longs for Anna Houba's body. And this is what really makes him think of converting to the denomination that receives the Sacrament in both kinds, this is still possible, yes, still possible. He will marry the deaf-mute Anna Houba in whose womb Vojtěch Paskal is already growing. What does it matter that he was expelled from St Anna's when he can hold Anna Houba in his arms every day, the silent Anna who smells of bread and coffee?

And then they take off together for Hradec, Anna is due at any moment, the slightest movement causes her difficulty. And Jan Paskal, who is supporting her, has a tiny groove around his neck left there by the clerical collar, a barely perceptible line, but at Luther's Institute nobody will mind it, not at Luther's Institute. How could Jan Paskal have made a good Catholic priest with so many Protestants among his ancestors? He even claims there existed a certain Jean de Pascal, a Huguenot who fled Paris the night of the St Bartholomew's Day Massacre. Paskal has Huguenot blood in his veins. What does it matter that it took Anna Houba to make it flow?

And years later, long after the deaf-mute Anna has turned to dust and ashes, and Nora Paskal is bringing up the growing Vojtěch, every time pastor Paskal administers the Sacrament and offers the faithful the body and blood of Christ (never forgetting to wipe the chalice with a napkin), he remembers another communion, the one with the bread and coffee of Anna Houba.

PASTRIES

Doctor Pelt is well aware that his daughter's mother is hiding behind the gazebo, and he finds this unpleasant. Although they are divorced now, his dislike for Nora's mother is not so intense as to make it impossible for him to endure her presence at least briefly. Her dress rustles from time to time anyway, and there is

14

also her shadow, which grows longer as the evening wears on. Ever present is the feeling of eternal guilt that Nora's mother makes so obvious to him, he senses it both in the shadow and in the rustling. Doctor Pelt wouldn't object to her sitting here now in the gazebo next to Nora, listening to his lecture on pruritus (itching) and on the 'vicious circle' generated by scratching.

She is still there as Pelt talks about purpura, even later on when he switches to psoriasis and ichthyosis, and even when he tries to explain to Nora the process of epidermal hardening — keratinization. Pelt was also going to lead up to leprosy (at the medical school he always introduced it by saying: In the Middle Ages, the term leprosy covered a wide range of skin diseases that modern medicine differentiates …), but the shadow cleaves to its place at all times, looming longer and longer, and suddenly Doctor Pelt loses all desire to broach his favourite subject, he gets up, kisses his daughter Nora's forehead, and sets off down the Babylonian path, freshly sprinkled with white sand in his honour. And as he walks along with his head bowed low so as to avoid meeting the shadow's glance, it suddenly seems to him it is not sand but flour that his daughter Nora's mother has intentionally sprinkled on the path as a silent reminder of his transgression.

That day she had also been sprinkling a path with flour — in a train, down the corridor of a second-class carriage. Lieutenant Pelt, an army doctor, stops her and says: Young lady, you won't get far with the flour that way. It was wartime flour, and had Lieutenant Pelt not offered to carry that flour out of the station for her through the officers' exit, and had he then not made her promise to bake him pastries from that flour, he probably would never have appeared at Koudelka & Co., manufacturers of mother-of-pearl buttons, to ask for her hand.

Doctor Pelt quickens his step, he is almost running along the Babylonian path sprinkled with ancient wartime flour. What if the shadow should suddenly start to run after him, trying to force upon him two fresh Babylonian pastries? And if he ate them, as he had once before, he could never leave Babylon again, he and his daughter Nora would stay there forever, beneath the lengthening shadow, held by a spell in the white gazebo of a rented garden.

THE UNICORN SCENE

She who is hiding behind the gazebo, who sprinkles the path with flour and white sand, who bakes pastries and whose lengthening shadow falls upon Pelt's head, is the eldest of six children (all genuinely historical Czech names: Libuše, Přemysl, Šárka, Ctirad, Ladislav and Vlasta), that's why it is she who every year accompanies her mummy, the future Mother-of-Pearl Queen, to the spa at Letiny near Blovice. One year in June the town puts up a triumphal arch to welcome its lord, Count Karl Schönborn, but Libuše only sees it from her window. That's because Mummy has disparaged it: That we should bow down to his lordship, like in the Middle Ages! Mummy is liberal-minded, despite being a lady and the wife of a factory owner. But what kind of a lady spends entire days sitting in the factory office and sometimes sews mother-of-pearl buttons onto pieces of cardboard with her children? This, however, she would never mention in the presence of Doctor Hart.

She who is casting furtive glances at the triumphal arch would like to run down, at least for a moment. Then she sees him step out of the carriage onto the road sprinkled with fresh white sand, shake hands with Doctor Hart and wave cordially to the spa guests. And she by the window feels as if he were waving to her, too. At that moment even Mummy herself steps over to the window to have a look at the petty count (the petty count, or Doctor Hart?), but doesn't refrain from disparaging the triumphal arch a second time.

Before evening sets in, a storm passes over Letiny, the splendour of the triumphal arch is reduced to nothing. Paper garlands and flowers, scattered in the mud of the spa's promenade, are drowning in puddles, and Doctor Hart's hunting dogs urinate on them. While Mummy lies in a peat bath, Libuše goes out. Now she may look at the triumphal arch, yes, now she may. Libuše passes back and forth under the triumphal arch. Count Schönborn's image still shimmers on the surface of the puddle, a scrap of crumpled paper floats across the count's face.

It floats across the face just as Mummy, resting in her peat bath, disparages the triumphal arch a third time. Doctor Hart is standing behind a screen. Colourful exotic birds descend upon paradisiacal trees and beneath their branches a white unicorn hides his head in the lap of a virgin. Doctor Hart, gazing at the scene, is overcome by a familiar feeling of envy and desire: if he were a unicorn, he would now hide his head in the lap of a virgin, at least for a moment, until the hunters catch up with him and slay him. Alas — if only that lap, that peat lap, were not so muddy.

On that very same day in June, in Sarajevo, conspirators assassinate the heir to the throne, the Archduke Ferdinand, and his spouse.

LITTLE HEADS MADE OF BREAD

Jan Paskal, he who married the deaf-mute, knows: somewhere in the flat are the little heads made of bread, those little heads of Christ sent to Anna by prisoners in gratitude for the food she hides for them in her shop (Anna sells tobacco and newspapers). Various people come by to pick up the food and then clandestinely pass it on to the prison. Maybe even the Germans who frequent Anna's shop know about this but won't tell because they like Anna Paskal's smile. Anna Paskal smiles, even though again somewhere under the counter she has several of those little heads made of bread, those little heads of Christ that she then takes home and randomly places wherever her fancy strikes. Anna Paskal isn't cautious enough, she thinks nothing can happen to her because Christ is always with her.

But Jan Paskal doesn't like this, he fears those little heads of the Saviour, those little heads that won't put an end to the war, but may put an end to Anna's life. She isn't even thinking of her son Vojtěch, no, not even of him, or what might happen to him. And this is what Jan Paskal keeps telling her, but Anna just goes on smiling and wondering, like a little child, why he, a pastor, wouldn't want to have Christ in his home.

And then one day, when Jan Paskal returns home from the village of Karhule near Blaník Mountain, where their son Vojtěch has been sent to live with farmer Tůňka's family, he finds the Hradec flat sealed. Jan Paskal understands: he has been proven right, those little heads have brought misfortune down upon Anna and won't save her now, those little heads constitute material evidence. How many little heads can there be in their home? This time Jan Paskal doesn't behave like a coward, no, not this time when he climbs through the neighbour's window into his own dwelling. For a moment, an abyss opens up beneath him. And then, inside his home, as Jan Paskal searches for Christ, yet another abyss opens up. He searches for Him for Anna's sake and for Vojtěch's sake (at least he took Vojtěch away to the country in time, to Karhule, where no German has ever set foot). And he also searches for Christ for his own sake. He keeps slipping the little heads, one after another, into his pockets, by now he has almost a dozen, but how many are still left, not even Anna could tell, no, not even she.

Yet one little head is left behind somewhere there, a little head of the one whose kingdom, according to the goatish prophecy, began in the year 1914. That little head will prove Anna guilty, Anna alone, Jan Paskal will get away, no one, surprisingly, is seeking Jan Paskal, no one, surprisingly, suspects Jan Paskal. And Jan Paskal, upon receiving Anna's death certificate and her worn shoes, leaves Hradec and goes to Prague.

I am the Olšany Cemetery. But I was also once the Syranov vineyard, little by little I yielded my ground to victims of the plague. My wine seeped deep into the Olšany soil, and the dead along with the earth inhale its fragrance. They abide here in a state of seemingly perpetual drunkenness, which only fleetingly, after enduring rains have flushed the wine away into deeper layers, changes into a hangover, into a bitter soberness. But as soon as the sun comes out, the wine begins to rise to the surface again, diffusing its intoxicating fragrance once more. Even the plague knaves breathe it in as they inter the dead. The earth begins to spin under their feet.

One of them must have gulped down too much of the wine-soaked soil, he still staggers among the graves at night, climbs over the wall and looks around for a long time before jumping down. But he is mistaken in thinking nobody sees him. Caretaker Briar sees him, for a whole month he has been watching him climb over the cemetery wall every other day and then come back. Caretaker Briar has recognized the man by now, no, he is not mistaken, it is Mr Klečka from their block of flats, the quiet gentleman from the third floor, who would have thought it. Caretaker Briar has also noticed that each time his coat seems to be oddly bulging, as if he were hiding something beneath it, by now Caretaker Briar is almost sure of it. And when Mr Klečka returns, there is no longer anything under his coat. The cemetery excursions of Mr Klečka keep Caretaker Briar awake at night. Who can Mr Klečka be going to see there every other day?

One night Caretaker Briar waits downstairs as Mr Klečka goes out, and stops him in the hallway for a chat. Mr Klečka has on his loden coat, a slightly shabby one, Caretaker Briar doesn't fail to notice. Nor does he fail to notice that, once again, the loden coat is strangely bulging. Caretaker Briar observes Mr Klečka's intense discomfort, how he wishes to be gone and already over the wall with his loden coat. But Caretaker Briar won't let him off so lightly and Mr Klečka doesn't dare show his impatience.

Caretaker Briar does not like people of Mr Klečka's and Mr Turk's sort, those two are living together. — What's the matter with Mr Turk? he asks Mr Klečka. — I haven't seen him in a long time, is he poorly, perhaps? And he drives the thorn deep into the flesh. Mr Klečka's shabby loden coat begins to tremble. It seems to bulge out even more than usual, and a strangely comical idea enters Caretaker Briar's mind: could it actually be Mr Turk hiding under Mr Klečka's loden coat? He dismisses the thought immediately but another one springs forth. There is a definite connection between Mr Klečka's loden coat and Mr Turk's disappearance. Some Mr Turk! Caretaker Briar knows full well, he has a nose for it, that Mr Turk never was and is no Turk, but just a common ordinary Jew. Caretaker Briar isn't easily fooled, let alone by some would-be Turk.

Meanwhile Mr Turk is waiting in a tomb. Outside, a melancholy angel watches over it, leaning his cheek on his hand (even he must have had one too many and his head has grown heavy from the Olšany wine). Mr Turk is waiting for Mr Klečka and worries about him, he's beginning to fear the worst. And when he can't bear it any longer, he goes to complain to his angel. But the angel, who probably tippled Olšany wine on an empty stomach, is in a daze and doesn't hear what Mr Turk is telling him. And in the meantime, in a flat with a window overlooking the cemetery, Mr Klečka has put his head down on the table, beside the bread he took from under his loden coat, and weeps.

The melancholy angel still lingers in his intoxication. Mr Klečka is familiar to him by now, the angel knows he comes here every other day to see Mr Turk and have long conversations with him. The angel hides the pair of them under his wings. Mr Turk slowly nibbles the bread while Mr Klečka tells him the latest news from beyond the wall. But just yesterday it happened that Mr Klečka didn't come, so Mr Turk has to content himself with only the angel's company. The November nights are chilly and Mr Turk's teeth are chattering. He doesn't even dare take his nightly walk among the graves. But the graves are vanishing, grapevines entwine trellises and grapes ripen before his eyes. They are dark and their heavy fragrance envelops Mr Turk, intoxicating him. However, he doesn't dare get up and pick a bunch of grapes. First I must eat bread and only then have wine, thinks Mr Turk. But he waits all through the night and the following day. It grieves him that the grapes are overripe by now, all blackened, and that there is a touch of putrefaction in their fragrance. Mr Turk begins to regret his decision to wait for Mr Klečka and the bread he brings, and that he hasn't tasted at least one grape.

Mr Klečka steals through the vineyard like a thief. Even the angel, who has awoken for a moment from his heavy slumber, notices that this time Mr Klečka is coming from the opposite direction. Tame squirrels scamper about his feet, and every now and then he throws them some breadcrumbs. Mr Turk doesn't touch the bread that night, he dreams only of grapes. He pushes Mr Klečka away as if he were angry with him for being late and letting the wine go bad. And Mr Klečka senses that Mr Turk is feverish and delirious.

And suddenly the vineyard is full of people and lights. And Mr Turk realizes that grape harvest time is nigh. The swollen grapes are bursting, their juice gushes forth and soaks into the ground. Even the angel lifts his head and suddenly turns sober. It would be fitting to enwreathe his head, like the head of Bacchus, thinks Mr Turk. But what kind of grape pickers are these, aren't they rather the plague knaves, they won't even spare the melancholy angel, not even the angel.

On the other side of the wall stands Caretaker Briar, shifting from one foot to the other. Of course he never dreamed it might come to the worst, of course not. — It's just that I'm concerned about the reputation of the block of flats, Herr Hergesell, the reputation of the block of flats.

Once more the three of them are sitting together — Mr Turk,

Mr Klečka and the melancholy angel with a wing missing. All around them are tame squirrels. Whenever they get together like this, which happens every other day to keep up the old habit, they talk about the same thing over and over again: what started it all, how Caretaker Briar stopped Mr Klečka at the bottom of the staircase just as he was going to see Mr Turk, and how, before Mr Turk's eyes, the cemetery was transformed into a vineyard, and how grape harvest time had come. The angel already knows their stories by heart. But what if the pickers were to come back some day, it occurs to Mr Turk, who confides his worry to Mr Klečka. Mr Klečka tries to comfort Mr Turk, no harm can come to departed souls any more, not any more, but Mr Turk doesn't believe him. One day Mr Klečka will see that Mr Turk was right. On the day they bring in the youth from the fiery furnace. Does Mr Turk mean the one who will set himself on fire one January day on Wenceslas Square, between the National Museum and the Food Bazaar? — Yes, that one. They will be afraid lest he should rise from the dead and so they will dig up the body and transfer it to Všetaty, his hometown. Not even the dead do they leave in peace, not even the dead. And yet again, Caretaker Briar will be standing on the other side of the wall, yet again.

So prophesies Mr Turk at Olšany. Everything repeats itself eternally. It is the same cycle as the grapes growing, ripening and being gathered by migrant pickers. Yesterday the pickers were still the plague knaves, but once the grapes are in, they'll pull their plague hoods back over their heads in place of the wine wreaths. Let Mr Klečka mark his words. But Mr Klečka shakes his head in disbelief over Mr Turk's tall tales. Grapes ripening here and wine pickers arriving to harvest them? — And whoever drinks the wine, yes, whoever so much as comes near it, says Mr Turk, turns into a plague knave himself.

Whenever Alice Davidovič rushes out to meet Pavel Santner, she must pass by Caretaker Briar's door on the ground floor. She tries to run by as quickly as possible so the caretaker won't glimpse her through his little window onto the hallway. But if Alice manages to slip by him on her way out, she is certain not to escape him on her way in. Caretaker Briar is standing in the doorway, pleading: Alice, do come in for a moment to play with our Georgie. And Alice has no choice but to go inside, where the smell of yesterday's cabbage promptly surrounds her. Already from the doorstep she can see Briar's son, Georgie, cursed into the form of an eternal child. Georgie is sitting on the sofa, his legs tucked under him, waiting.

Caretaker Briar invites Alice to sit down next to Georgie. After sitting on the sofa next to Georgie for a while, Alice usually can't come up with anything better than to suggest they go together to Bubeník's pub for a soda. Georgie likes soda very much. This is Georgie's greatest venture into a world stretching from the sofa to the silvery counter that mesmerizes him. And the soda itself excites Georgie to the depths of his soul, he holds the cool glass to his ear and listens to the water fizzing, while furtively watching the bubbles rising from the bottom to the surface where they disappear. Georgie tries to prolong endlessly this vertiginous moment of fizzing and bubbling and disappearing before he swallows the miraculous water in a few hasty gulps that burn his throat. He also dallies because he likes to observe his matt image reflected in the shiny surface of the counter. And sometimes, when Georgie takes too long, the bubbles fizzle out and the water's fire no longer burns his throat. It is the soda's fate that teaches Georgie about the transience of things. He feels cheated and puts the blame on Alice.

When winter comes, Georgie finds himself another pastime. He watches from the window for Alice to return, and then runs out the moment he sees her and asks her to let him put his hand inside her muff, just to warm it a little. Alice nods and Georgie slips his hand inside, nestling his palm over the back of hers. Alice thinks only of how soon she'll be able to go home, and when she feels the muff game has gone on too long, she pulls her hand out of the muff to signal the warming ritual is over.

One day Pavel Santner walks Alice all the way home, Alice holds Pavel Santner's hand to make sure he won't change his mind and try to leave. This time Alice isn't carrying her Persian lamb muff, it's Pavel Santner who has it. Alice hasn't thought of Georgie even once that day, how could she have, when she senses herself still in Pavel Santner's arms, feeling as if a new Davidovič has already begun to grow inside her? But Georgie does see Alice on that day, on that day even better than on other days, he doesn't come out but his eyes keep following her, even through the little window onto the hallway. He also sees that Alice's muff isn't in its usual place, and that confuses him. He tries to talk to his father about this, saying: someone has taken Alice Davidovič's muff. Caretaker Briar understands this to mean that someone has stolen the little Jewish girl's muff. — What a waste of a muff, he thinks, it was Persian lamb.

The following day, when Alice returns home, Caretaker Briar informs Georgie that she has her muff back again. And once more Alice's hands are in the muff, hiding away from the world, from the world above all, since the winter is by no means severe. And suddenly Georgie is there, facing Alice, begging. Alice nods and his hand slips inside. Georgie Briar has a pin, he stabs it into Alice's hand. For the son, like the father, yearns to have a thorn of his own.

And what if Alice Davidovič had died already then, at the moment the pin stabbed her hand, what if Georgie Briar had cursed her as punishment for letting Pavel Santner carry her muff? For Alice the whole world then changed before her eyes. This didn't happen right away, of course, only after a while, when the briar poison had permeated her entire body. One day she entered the pantry and in the pantry was Grandfather Davidovič, he had risen from the dead that day, and Alice let herself believe that Pavel Santner would come, although until then she had known for certain that he had left with a transport. But suddenly there was that onion Pavel Santner had brought, Grandfather Davidovič was peeling it and making Grandmother cry. And then Alice decided to go and meet Pavel Santner, she often used to do that, though Grandmother kept telling her not to. Only this time she didn't go the usual way — down the stairs and then up the path along the cemetery — instead she stepped out of the window, she was so very eager.

When Alice was exactly halfway between heaven and earth, between her childhood room and the cemetery, she seemed to feel Pavel Santner bending over her, and right then, the life of a new Davidovič was conceived within her. At that moment Alice grew somewhat frightened, wondering whether the flight might not endanger the child, but then she calmed down. As children, hadn't they always jumped off the cemetery wall, backwards and with their eyes shut, and always landed in the soft soil, sinking their fingers into it? The earth seemed to smell of some exotic fruit and they wanted to see how it tasted.

But at that moment Alice failed to realize that a body falls straight down and thus could never fly across the road. And all that because a briar thorn had pricked her hand and left a tiny red mark.

THE HART FROM BLANÍK MOUNTAIN

Jan Paskal is a saint, he took in a deaf-mute orphan, made her his wife, he converted for the sake of a deaf-mute girl. Saint Jan Paskal, Nora Pelt's mother calls him. And during these difficult war years, Saint Jan Paskal brings pork lard to the ailing Nora Pelt. One day he even brings her a hart. A hart should be left to cure, Nora Pelt's mother thinks, Mummy would have let it cure. And so the hart is put out on the balcony. And while Saint Paskal sits at the sick girl's bedside, the hart rests in brine on the balcony. It is no ordinary hart, farmer Tůňka slew it on Blaník Mountain.

And what were all those stories that Tůňka was telling, about how he lost his way while hunting and entered the mountain where they say there are knights seated at a round table, asleep, and the hart, white as snow, fled all the way into the mountain, came to the table and ate leftovers from that table and finished wine left in the goblets. Maybe it was no ordinary hart but an enchanted youth, such a hart, what a pity, but war is war, no one is spared, not even magical harts. And the magical harts then lie in brine on the balcony, they've already been lying there a number of days, while inside Jan Paskal is wooing his second wife, placing his head in her lap.

The ailing Nora Pelt finds this odd: the clergyman places his head in her lap, and it exudes the scent of church. Nora Pelt bends down to his head, its scent excites her. She has no way of knowing this is the scent of Kain, the scent of the theatre, for she cannot yet tell the difference, not yet. Just as long as there will never be any little heads made of bread, not even a single one, like the one that was left behind, and then a single pair of shoes, nothing more.

A year later, when Nora returns home from the tuberculosis sanatorium, they celebrate a wedding. The eminent Doctor Pelt himself is present. Even at the wedding reception he cannot resist giving his lecture on skin. And he keeps casting anxious glances because a certain shadow falls across his forehead. He senses her standing somewhere behind one of the columns — the mother of Nora Pelt and her four unborn siblings. Just as long as she doesn't sprinkle the floor with flour, the flour would swirl up under the feet of the wedding guests, it would settle on their clothes, even on the fur coat of the second Mrs Pelt. It is mid-April, yet the second Mrs Pelt keeps shivering with cold beneath her two fur coats, her beaver and the one made from the words *de morbis cutaneis*, for her there is a winter garden all around.

At the reception the woman behind the column remembers the magical hart, how she soaked it in brine and then roasted it. The hart had quite decomposed, perhaps the brine wasn't properly prepared or else that piece, the magical hart from Blaník Mountain, was too old. It should have stayed inside the mountain eating leftovers from the table and finishing the wine. The hart's meat was not edible, due either to the brine or the mountain, which opened up in time of war, only to supply a useless piece. And that's what would probably happen even with the knights, should they come out in Bohemia's darkest hour, even with St Wenceslas on a white charger at their head. They would all be old and useless, and return into the mountain to dwell there for evermore.

A WOLF IN THE TEMPLE OF THE LORD

Suffer little children to come unto me. The door of the Lord's temple is open, it is open to everyone, Pastor Paskal's sheep enter through it one at a time, and among them a black sheep, Herr Hergesell. The frightened sheep make way for him. This is no sheep, this is a wolf in sheep's clothing. Behold, the wolf is coming to the temple for the body and blood of the Lord, he eats the bread and drinks the wine together with the sheep. Huddled in a tight little flock, the sheep are slowly sidling toward the door of the temple, and then, one by one, begin to vanish into the wintry night, until finally the wolf is left alone with the clergyman. He is humble and quiet, as if he wanted to lay his head in the clergyman's lap and repent. — This is a tame wolf, Pastor Paskal thinks to himself in the sacristy, as he unbuttons his collar with trembling fingers. Why, it's only Herr Hergesell from their block of flats, they say he's a court clerk, just a court clerk, nothing more. Through a crack in the door Paskal sees the wolf slowly get up and approach him. He stops at the threshold, saying nothing, just looking.

At home Jan Paskal tells his wife: Today I gave the Eucharist to the German from our block of flats. He's just a court clerk ... — You think so? Nora Paskal replies. — They don't all wear uniforms. Jan Paskal knows that too. And it occurs to him: I'm just like Judas, I've delivered Christ to Pilate but don't have the courage to hang myself. If only Jan Paskal could have known all that was to happen next, over the course of several months. Judas would move into Pilate's residence. And that wouldn't be the end of it. Should he perhaps have driven him from the temple? Paskal felt sorry for his sheep, they wouldn't have had enough time to make it across to the other side of the abyss. He won't admit, however, that he also felt sorry for himself, even he wouldn't have had enough time to cross to the other side, as pastor he would have been the last to go.

At night Jan Paskal prays to God, but He will not comfort him for He is the Protestant God, relentless and severe. Instead of God, it is Herr Hergesell from the fifth floor who reveals himself to him, he puts out his hand and Pastor Paskal places a host in his palm. But this is a sacrilege, for the second time in one day he betrays Christ. Yet what is he to do when there are sheep all around him? The bread and wine will tame the wolf, he'll be sated and go on his way. Wolf Hergesell stands on the threshold of the sacristy, bowing. All of a sudden he jumps inside, snatches the clergyman's collar and runs away with it. A frightening image comes to Jan Paskal's mind: what if the wolf puts on the collar and the unsuspecting sheep follow him one by one? That has already happened, the streets are filled with their pitiful bleating. Jan Paskal looks outside. The Olšany Cemetery is all white — is it snow or white fleece, what do you think, Pastor Paskal?

THE SUPPER

Herr Hergesell, the court clerk from the fifth floor, worries Jan Paskal. On every Holy Day he comes to listen to the sermon and, without confessing his sins, receives the Holy Eucharist from Pastor Paskal. Already twice Herr Hergesell has penetrated Pastor Paskal's sacristy to discuss communion in both kinds. This man has virtually forced himself into the ranks of the Bohemian Protestant flock (by accepting the Reformation, he says, Bohemia has already joined the German Empire), and now he's on the lookout for a sacrificial lamb.

What a strange friendship — Herr Hergesell, a court clerk, and Jan Paskal, a Protestant minister. They share the same view from the windows of their flats, beneath them both lies the same abyss: the Olšany Cemetery. Evidently, this circumstance has brought them together — against their wills, or at least against the will of one of them. And one day Herr Hergesell greets his downstairs neighbour and asks out of the blue: So, Pastor, have you found Christ yet? And Jan Paskal senses an allusion to the little head of Christ made of bread, the one he didn't find, the one that sent Anna Houba flying out of the chimney in Poland.

Jan Paskal continues on his way without answering. He doesn't even say that the search for Christ is unending, for a believer continues to discover Christ within himself but can never find him completely, because at that point he would become one with Christ, he himself would become Christ. This is Paskal's belief, undoubtedly rather heretical, but quite in keeping with his own way of thinking — always on the brink of orthodoxy and heresy. The boundary is so vague, after all. But the little head, the little head of the Son of God, made of bread, he can't get it out of his mind.

The next time they meet, Herr Hergesell turns the conversation to Mr Turk. — Where's our Mr Turk gone, Pastor, don't you know anything about him? Paskal knows, or rather suspects that Mr Turk is in hiding, Mr Klečka is so utterly unable to lie, one can read him like an open book. Jan Paskal also knows that every other day Mr Klečka carries something somewhere. Herr Hergesell seems to know about this too, that's why his question comes across at the same time as an accusation. Herr Hergesell must be waiting for someone to denounce those two men, but it won't be Jan Paskal, Jan Paskal is not an informer, not yet. On the contrary, he goes to warn Mr Klečka the very same day. But Herr Hergesell mustn't find out, most likely this is all a trap and Jan Paskal has just fallen into it.

Mr Klečka, naturally, cannot stop his errands, how can he let Mr Turk die of hunger just like that? Jan Paskal understands, he presses Mr Klečka's hand firmly, even though up to now he had never cared much for Mr Klečka, nor had he ever cared much for Mr Turk, but now he has allied himself with them, and Herr Hergesell will certainly not fail to notice. After Paskal's warning, Mr Klečka is even more frightened and it becomes even more obvious that he's hiding something, Caretaker Briar is already lying in wait for him at the foot of the stairs. And Jan Paskal is responsible for this, though he won't admit as much.

Then one day in the beginning of May, Herr Hergesell invites the Paskals for supper at his place. — We're neighbours, after all. My home is so empty without the family, Herr Hergesell says, looking meaningfully at Nora Paskal, as if trying to win her sympathy. Or has he already won it?

Herr Hergesell has made a lamb roast for supper. — You don't mind, Pastor Paskal, eating yourself? Herr Hergesell takes pride in his classical education and expands on the etymology of Paskal's name: paschalis — paschal. A lamb — what else? It's a bad joke and not even Nora Paskal laughs, though she has always loathed lamblike creatures and found wolves more interesting. She even pulls her leg away at the touch of the wolf's paw.

There is already a platter on the table, and on that platter are slices of bread. Everybody takes a piece — Nora Paskal, Jan Paskal and, finally, the host himself, Herr Hergesell. And beneath the last slice lies a bread crumb. The longer Jan Paskal stares at it, the better he recognizes the features of the divine countenance, shrivelled and disfigured by time, by wartime. No, this isn't a bread crumb, this is a little head, the head of the aged Saviour, who no longer brings salvation, but perdition instead. Jan Paskal feels Herr Hergesell's eyes riveted on him, both he and Nora already know about the little head, they are both looking at the countenance of the transformed Saviour.

Suddenly Jan Paskal gathers his courage and covers the crumb with a white paper napkin, as one covers a corpse with a sheet. And that's precisely what Herr Hergesell has been waiting for, precisely for that, because this confirms the identity of what until then had been a mere bread crumb, nothing more. Behold, the miracle of the Lord's transubstantiation, Herr Hergesell says, and raises...

Grandfather and Grandmother Davidovič are dozing off in the pantry when a quarrel breaks out in the flat, but their sleep is light because they are waiting for Alice, who has gone to meet Pavel Santner. That it has been three years since she left doesn't seem to disturb them. A different sense of time reigns in the pantry — cosmic time, in which night and day are indistinguishable.

— Something is going on in there, it sounds like a fight. Grandmother Davidovič is standing by the door, pressing her ear to it. — A pastor isn't allowed to fight. — He's a Lutheran, Grandfather Davidovič says and gives a wry laugh.

And then the door opens, and a lifeless body falls in. It slumps to the floor with a thud, stirring up the ancient dust, almost making Grandfather Davidovič sneeze.

THE REVOLUTION

I am the revolution. I am the revolution at Hradčany Castle and the revolution at Olšany, I am the revolution in Lobkowicz Square, the revolution in Kouřim Street, and I am even a very small revolution in Zásmuky Lane — that's the narrow lane perpendicular to the cemetery wall.

I am the revolution in flats where glass cabinets with Bohemian crystal are moved into entryways so that the crystal may endure the revolution. When there's shooting, the crystal rings softly, but endures.

I am the revolution in the shops — I am taking down the German signboards. Mr Poustka, the grocer, takes down his sign, and after him Mr Širc, the butcher, and after him Mr Trnka, the delicatessen owner, and after him Mr Bubeník, the pub owner (he's the one whose pub Alice and Georgie would go to for sodas)

— then, for a long time, nobody — until finally the very last one, doubting Thomas Hamza, the tobacconist, takes his sign down too. And only then, after the time of taking down signs, after the period of changing names (because names are of primary importance in every revolution), I begin to set up barricades. — One barricade on Foch Avenue (formerly Jungmann, later Schwerin, then Stalin, finally Vinohradská Avenue), another barricade in Kouřim Street, and a very small barricade in Zásmuky Lane. Then, for the next three days, shots are fired from the cemetery in the direction of the school, and from the school back in the direction of the cemetery. For three days Jan Köck (he's Czech, not a German) sleeps next to his glass cabinet with Bohemian crystal. The crystal rings softly, but endures. Mr Köck endures too.

I am also the revolution in the cellars, the hidden one. I'm in charge of a purge separating the wheat from the chaff. I ask the chaff to step forward and then gather and transport them to Hagibor, formerly a Jewish Home, after that a German torture chamber. Instruments of torture are still there, left behind by the Germans — racks for torturing Jews, Grandfather Davidovič among them, and wheels for breaking Jews' limbs one at a time, including those of Grandfather Davidovič (he shouldn't have been going to Mrs Soška's). And Mr Böhm, chaff Böhm, steps forward in the cellar, and so does chaff Vinkler (now actually Winkler) — all the other tenants, pure wheat every one of them, gasp in astonishment. Who would believe that Mr Vinkler, that nice gentleman, is a German? Even Mr Vinkler, chaff Winkler, will be taken to Hagibor by me, the revolution, currently embodied in Caretaker Briar. Mr Vinkler, chaff Winkler, is racked, the limbs of Mr Vinkler, of chaff Winkler, are broken, one at a time. — Chaff is chaff, says Caretaker Briar, himself also pure wheat, as he waves a red-blue-and-white flag atop a truck that shuttles to and from Hagibor.

I am the revolution and I am victorious at Olšany, I am victorious in Lobkowicz Square (it will become Chapaev Square), I am victorious in Kouřim Street and I am even victorious in the narrow Zásmuky Lane. Female chaff remove dead bodies from the sidewalk, bodies flushed out of houses during the revolution, they're sweeping away the revolutionary residue. Nearby, in front of the pharmacy, in whose shiny dark façade Georgie Briar will admire his own reflection, loiters Mr Köck, pure wheat, not chaff, despite his weed-like name. Suddenly Mr Köck picks up a wooden beam and starts to hit Mrs Vinkler, chaff Winkler, on the head. Tenants at windows facing the square, and also Mr Hamza who has to lean quite far out in order to see all the way to the pharmacy, gasp in astonishment: Who would have expected this from Mr Köck, of all people, Mr Köck who plays the cello at the National Theatre, who would believe it's the same Mr Köck who just a few days ago greeted Mrs Vinkler at the tobacconist's with 'I kiss your hand, madam'?

I am the revolution, the purifying element and the distinguishing element, the transforming element and the reversing element. Behold Caretaker Briar, only yesterday he was pointing his finger at the cemetery wall (merely concerned for the well-being and reputation of the block of flats he's in charge of), but today he attends to the revolution, waving its flag up high. Behold doubting Thomas Hamza, only yesterday he was filled with uncertainty, but now, having thrust his hand into the revolution's wound, he recites a prayer in the presence of every customer: Our Revolution, Thy will be done. Behold the body (somewhat fat) and the blood of Mr Köck. Only yesterday... but today, despite his weed-like name, Mr Köck (or is it Mr Cockle by now?) is undergoing the most miraculous of all revolutionary reincarnations. And the nation receives the body and blood of Mr Köck, for the nation professes the faith that receives the Sacrament in both kinds.

Residing in the pantry, Grandmother and Grandfather Davidovič only experience the revolution filtered through the lightwell. For them, the revolution is connected with the body that appeared one day in the middle of the pantry floor, and which Grandmother Davidovič later dragged with great difficulty under the bed, because it was in her way. They're convinced the revolution with which the war had ended (at least around here at Olšany) was actually the quarrel that took place in the flat, a quarrel between a German court clerk and a Czech pastor, resulting in the death of one of them. They considered the noise from the street, which for several days they heard distantly through the lightwell, to be merely the aftermath of that row.

— I just don't understand, Grandmother Davidovič says to Grandfather Davidovič on 9 May, 1945, why nobody seems to be interested in this dead man here. With all the commotion they must have forgotten about him.

Herr Hergesell, whose soul is huddling in the farthest corner under the bed, realizes they're talking about him and huddles more tightly. It was not pleasant to discover himself so utterly defenceless in his present state, and totally at the mercy of the two Jews plotting to get rid of him. Incidentally, he also thought that the street shooting was directly connected with him. He is troubled by the realization that even if somebody should come upstairs into the pantry, only his body would be taken away, while his soul would be left to that malicious old couple. He has no choice but to try and escape on his own. Herr Hergesell peeks out from under the bed but immediately crawls back upon encountering Grandfather Davidovič's glare.

— We need his company like the dickens, Grandfather Davidovič says. — He'll settle in for good and eat our bread. Herr Hergesell under the bed is quiet as a mouse. — What if Alice brings Pavel Santner today? He'd never set foot in here again.

Saddened by it all, Grandmother Davidovič finally comes up with a brilliant idea. How about trying to open the lightwell window, maybe the unpleasant guest would fly out through there. And indeed, as soon as Herr Hergesell feels the air (mixed with a bit of gunpowder smoke) he cautiously slithers out from under the bed, shakes off the dust and lifts off into the lightwell.

Flying is a new and strange experience for him, and so is looking down from a bird's or rather a soul's perspective. And what he sees down below is strange too. Barricades of junk block the streets, dead bodies sprawl on the pavement, and tanks move slowly through the city, from up high they look like beetles. And then he spots a lanky young man coming down the street along the Olšany Cemetery and entering the very house Herr Hergesell has just left. It must be Pavel Santner, the one they had talked about.

And it is indeed Pavel Santner. He walks past Caretaker Briar, who is standing in the hallway clad in a mouse-grey overcoat, and goes up to the fifth floor. And things go exactly as Grandfather Davidovič had feared. Pavel Santner enters the pantry but promptly backs out and hurries away. Grandfather Davidovič was right to think he would be put off. How could he, under such circumstances, ask for Alice's hand? This way all will again be postponed until God knows when. What on earth will they tell Alice when she returns? She has been so looking forward to this moment.

And now Alice is here, she's rushing into the pantry all out of breath. She has on her best dress, its white collar is a little wrinkled. Of course Alice knows who has been here. And they couldn't get Pavel Santner to stay even for a moment? But how could they have? Alice feels like bursting into tears but is ashamed to do so before Grandfather and Grandmother. — Come now, dearie, Grandmother Davidovič tries to console her, since you've waited all through the war, you can wait a little while longer. But Alice knows that by then she'll have grown old and ugly like Grandmother Davidovič, and Pavel Santner won't want her any more.

A VICTORY CELEBRATION

Caretaker Briar has guests. He invited them himself to celebrate the victory together. Platon Lvovich Glinka and Kostya Sukhoruchkov are sitting on the sofa. Georgie, with his legs tucked under him, sits enthroned between them. That was some shooting that went on in the Olšany Cemetery! And the squirrels, as if crazed by the shooting, crawled into the tombs with the marksmen and scampered about their feet. Maybe they were expecting some bits of bread from them, as from Mr Klečka. Towards midday, the melancholy angel lost a hand, and his head, deprived of its support, now absurdly juts out into space, tilted to one side.

Kostya Sukhoruchkov also suffered a wounded hand, his arm hangs in a sling made from a checkered scarf that reminds Georgie of Alice Davidovič's muff. Kostya Sukhoruchkov uses his good hand to cut slices off a lamb salami and feeds them to Georgie. This is Georgie's Holy Communion.

They drink a toast to victory. They drink a toast to Glinka. — Briar, do you know Glinka? Platon Lvovich here is his descendant. Caretaker Briar knows Glinka, he likes his music, he likes Platon Lvovich too. But Caretaker Briar is rather restless, he keeps jumping up at the slightest sound from the staircase, he keeps peering out through the little window into the hallway. Caretaker Briar would bet his life that Herr Hergesell didn't leave his flat during the revolution, and for some reason this makes Caretaker Briar uneasy. What if Herr Hergesell should suddenly decide to come down and ring Briar's doorbell, what if he should ask Caretaker Briar to hide him in his apartment? And then Caretaker Briar comes up with a brilliant idea: he'll send the two Russians upstairs, telling them a Kraut may still be hiding there. Platon Lvovich Glinka and Kostya Sukhoruchkov promptly jump up from the sofa, making Georgie, who is sitting between them, bounce up, and they charge upstairs. Caretaker Briar can hear them trying to force their way into the flat. And then nothing, silence, no shooting. And in no time they are back again, Kostya Sukhoruchkov with a happy grin points to his throat, someone had slaughtered the German like a suckling pig. Platon Lvovich pats Briar on the shoulder, Briar's nation and he are fine fellows.

And then Caretaker Briar ceremoniously produces a record book in which he notes complaints from tenants, and asks them to sign their names in it as a souvenir. Their entry happens to fall on a page following the request for a new bathtub from a certain Mr Hergesell, fifth floor. Toward morning, as the guests get up from the sofa (Georgie fell asleep long ago, his head resting in Kostya's lap), they kiss Caretaker Briar good-bye. By kissing Briar's forehead, Platon Lvovich Glinka kisses the whole nation.

After they have gone, Caretaker Briar pulls out his record book of complaints and carefully tears out the next to last page. You, Hergesell, would have done better requesting a coffin, Briar muses and chuckles at his own joke. As he settles down on the sofa next to Georgie for a short predawn nap, Caretaker Briar notices that mixed with the odour of yesterday's cabbage there is now the smell of Platon Lvovich's Russian tobacco and a whiff of iodine from Kostya Sukhoruchkov's bandaged hand. And also a slight smell of American chocolate, from a piece left lying on the table.

BABYLON

Nora Paskal divides everything between her two sons into equal shares, shares perhaps too equal to allow Vojtěch, the older of the two, to forget she is his stepmother. She divides into equal shares both her caring and her indifference, but that won't change a thing, later on she will still be branded a harsh stepmother, and she'll also take on the role of an adulteress.

Nora Paskal is not devout. She is the daughter of the renowned dermatologist Pelt who, while priding himself on his Protestantism, has really always worshipped only one deity: the Skin. Nora Pelt spent all her youth in the shadow of the Skin. At the foot of Babylon Mountain, where she and her mother used to spend summers, the three of them would sometimes sit in white wicker chairs in the garden gazebo. She and her mother both listened piously as Pelt talked about his Skin. And as the stream of words *de morbis cutaneis* flowed by, they would take sips of the ever cooler tea, together with the gossamer in the late summer air. And the wood of the gazebo, heated by the sun, smelled sweet. Nora Pelt always felt an urge to tear down the screen of skin separating her from Pelt (that's what she called her father), to interrupt the speech after which he always hastily rose to leave, to keep him in the gazebo, him and the passing summer.

The first winter after the war Nora Pelt feels homesick for Babylon. She travels there and sets out to look for the gazebo with its white chairs. Quite surely Pelt is still seated in one of them, surely he hasn't noticed that summer has ended, autumn has passed, and now it is winter. The grass around the gazebo is gone, as is the well-worn path leading to it, instead there is a blanket of pristine snow. Nora Paskal runs away from home, leaving behind even the baby Diviš, and takes off for Babylon to join Pelt. A law student by the name of Bark (who insists they had already met once long ago, possibly in a past life), joins her along the way and accompanies her to the foot of Babylon Mountain. Needless to say, Bark has no idea that he has arrived in a chosen place, that in the centre of the garden there is a little island where an eternal Babylonian summer reigns even now in wintertime. They wander in the garden till they reach the gazebo, Bark calls it the Tower of Babel and laughs at his own joke.

The gazebo slants to one side, as if it were about to collapse any moment. Here and there some of its boards have been pried off, for the gazebo is no longer a gazebo, once more it has become mere wood that kept the fires going in the Babylonian furnaces during wartime winters. Pelt is not there, but his chair is pushed back as if he had just got up upon hearing them coming. Perhaps he would have stayed had Nora come alone, had Bark not laughed so loudly at his own witticism. Nora Pelt's soul shivers with cold and anxiety caused by the Babylonian misunderstanding that arose from the confusion of tongues.

There is yet another confusion of tongues — during a kiss whose bitterness Nora Paskal tastes immediately afterwards. Then and there she is transformed into a whore of Babylon. And now Nora is astride an apocalyptic beast. She calls to Pelt for help but he doesn't hear her calling, at that very moment he is standing among a throng of disciples, delivering a lecture on the Skin, *de morbis cutaneis.*

THE SKIN

I am the skin. I am not, however, just any skin, but human skin. I am the protective peel, the shell that protects the body, like a rare fruit, from the light. Were it not for me, man in his folly would be capable of letting his body dissolve into the world. I am the barrier that keeps the body within its corporeality. As long as I exist, the body lasts, should I begin to decay, the body is also doomed to decay. I am the skin. Through me two beings briefly meet, only to walk immediately along a snow-covered path, each alone, leaving behind a smouldering Babylonian misunderstanding. The rubbing of skin against skin, referred to as pleasure, has nothing to do with the soul that I protect, and that is everywhere and nowhere.

I am the skin of babies born during the first postwar winter, soft as the silk secreted by bodies of silkworms. I am the skin of little Diviš. One day my softness will arouse the envy of the hunchbacked maid Anežka who will twist the baby's forearm till it burns. That will be his first St Bartholomew's Massacre.

I am the skin of dermatologists, dozens upon dozens of samples from the living and the dead. — Why don't you take us along to the leprosarium one of these days, Pelt? But I am also the skin of saints, among them St Bartholomew, the patron saint of butchers and tanners, bookbinders, glovers, shoemakers, and tailors. In an engraving the saint has me draped over his arm like a purple cloak in which he felt too hot. I am cast-off skin renewing itself like a snake's skin.

I am the skin of Jan Paskal, I am hanging in the pantry, in an old wardrobe saturated with moth repellent, crushed from all sides by faded, outmoded clothes. I do not shrink, I do not shrivel up like the skin of the fairytale donkey, quite the contrary: I grow bigger and stronger every year, thus I feel more and more cramped in here. The key to the wardrobe is in the sole possession of father Paskal, the children are not allowed in here. This is to keep them from turning me loose like Death. Inscribed on the door of the wardrobe are the letters A.D. — Anno Domini, meaning the year of the Lord, father Paskal tells them when they ask. And maybe he thinks he's telling them the truth, though the date is missing. The children, however, interpret the inscription in their own way: the wardrobe belongs to Anna Domina, she left it in their safekeeping and will come back for it some day.

I am the skin. I am hanging in here, hypertrophying. And on a certain day of the year strange patterns appear on my surface — the designs from Grandmother Davidovič's tablecloth.

ALL SOULS' SUNDAY

Pavel Santner is walking along the Olšany Cemetery, damp with All Souls' Day. He has turned up the collar of his winter coat, lest one of the obtrusive souls should fly down inside his shirt collar and chill his back somewhere between his shoulder blades. Pavel Santner hasn't the slightest notion that souls seek out completely different ways and don't approach the living like raindrops but rather like dust motes that penetrate into children's rooms and pantries through ill-fitting windows. By early morning, some of the souls have already slipped into flats, where they rub against one another and against the floor, as if trying to kindle a spark of life. They keep lamenting and arguing among themselves about which of them has it worse.

The Paskals' flat on the fifth floor is full of souls, it is but a short way from the cemetery, and for a soul to ascend is easier than for a body to descend. (It is the same flat where the Hergesells had stayed earlier and before them the Davidovičes. — Who else but you should have it now, Mr Paskal, you acted like a hero, it's a large flat and you have two children, Caretaker Briar said.) For the souls, a pastor's flat is the Promised Land. But Mařenka Tůňka knows nothing about this. Unsuspecting, she opens the window in the children's room and shakes out lace doilies. A whole flock of souls flies in at once. Grandmother Davidovič examines them through a crack in the door, trying to see if Mrs Soška is among them. Grandfather Davidovič laughs at the idea: How can she be here when she hasn't died yet? But Grandmother doesn't quite trust Grandfather's word.

— Why, Grandmother, is today the Sabbath? asks Grandfather upon noticing that Grandmother is looking for the holiday tablecloth. And Grandmother Davidovič chides Grandfather for having forgotten who is coming to see them today: Alice is bringing Pavel Santner, isn't she?

Pavel Santner stops in front of the house and looks up, not noticing Alice Davidovič, who is waiting just a few steps away from him. There is no way he could notice her, but Alice feels hurt just the same. Pavel Santner sees a girl leaning out of the window of Alice's room, the girl is holding something white in her hand and waving. Pavel Santner is shortsighted and thus not sure whether she is waving to him. And then he sees something white fluttering down, a small handkerchief or a sheet of paper? Pavel Santner squints his straining eyes. He hears a cry — from the one upstairs who is waving to him, or from the other one standing motionless beside him? He doesn't even suspect that the white cloth caught in the branches of the tree has just traced the path travelled by Alice's falling body.

If the tree trunk had not been so damp, and Pavel Santner not so tightly bundled in his winter coat, he might have tried to climb up. But he feels embarrassed before the people coming and going — to their graves and back from their graves. Pavel Santner stands helplessly under the tree, not knowing that Alice Davidovič is two steps away from him, waiting for him to make up his mind. Then, suddenly, the girl from upstairs appears, Mařenka Tůňka, who is now the Paskals' maid. She puts her arms around the tree trunk and begins to climb up, while people are coming and going, back from their graves and to their graves, and Pavel Santner keeps

41

standing under the tree, the collar of his winter coat upturned.

Now with the white cloth in hand, Mařenka Tůňka is climbing down. The tree trunk is damp with All Souls' Day, and Alice Davidovič is waiting nearby, as if rooted to the ground. She has completely forgotten that she's forbidden to be out after dark, even in the company of Pavel Santner. And in the pantry, Grandfather and Grandmother Davidovič are waiting for her in vain. Suddenly Mařenka Tůňka's foot slips and her body falls. It must be Alice's doing, she has cast a spell on her because she is jealous that Mařenka Tůňka is alive and Pavel Santner is looking at her. And now Pavel Santner is bending over Mařenka Tůňka, he touches her foot, then lifts her up and carries her upstairs, leaving Alice Davidovič's soul behind in the rain, never realizing she might perhaps dissolve in it. And what if Pavel Santner thinks it is she — Alice, he will carry her upstairs to Grandfather and Grandmother Davidovič and not even they will realize it isn't Alice, and Pavel Santner will ask Grandfather for her hand and Grandfather will give him his blessing. That's what he had wanted to do once before, long ago, but something had prevented it then, Alice can't recall just now what it was.

It would seem the easiest thing in the world for a soul to flutter its wings and fly off, it would even seem much easier than for a body to undertake a free fall. But perhaps because Alice Davidovič is drenched from the rain and her wings have grown heavy with water, she is unable to lift off the ground. She feels her disembodied self slowly dissolving in the rain. She should have listened to Grandmother after all and not gone to meet Pavel Santner. She makes it too obvious how deeply she cares for him, and that's just why she has lost him, that's just why — for the second time now.

That day the pantry was a much livelier place than usual, the noise could be heard as far as the children's room. At times it sounded as if someone were opening the wardrobe, rummaging in it and then closing it again. The noises grew louder as Mařenka Tůňka ran downstairs. Then it even sounded as if someone were moving furniture in the pantry, perhaps shifting the table from under the lightwell window to a different place. That was when Grandmother Davidovič (actually her soul, since Grandmother Davidovič had flown out of a chimney somewhere in Poland) was returning the table to its original place because she was expecting Alice and her fiancé Pavel Santner. For the longest time she couldn't find the Sabbath tablecloth — hence all the rustling — and suspected Grandfather had hidden it somewhere intentionally. But Grandfather Davidovič in his corner just went on wryly laughing.

When the noise in the pantry wouldn't stop, Vojtěch sent little Diviš to see what was going on there. Suppose a fight had broken out between the Chamberlain and the Chambermaid, maybe they can both exist simultaneously and the presence of one doesn't preclude the presence of the other. But Vojtěch was just saying that, in reality, he no longer believed in the bird-rat because he was now almost grown up. In reality it occurred to him that a beggar might have broken into the pantry. Maybe the two men who had eaten lunch with them today were hiding in there. For it was a custom in Jan Paskal's home to invite beggars to luncheon every Sunday. Even today Vojtěch and Diviš had given them nicknames, calling one Mortar because he rattled his spoon against the plate, and the other Wild Boar because of his teeth. Vojtěch has been thinking about the two visitors, about Mortar and Wild Boar, ever since lunch. They struck him as being too humble, a bit too much. He also noticed that their way of constantly glancing about the flat, as if they were looking for something, made his father nervous. And at the table they were saying strange things and stopped only after his father told them he wasn't interested in politics. Jan Paskal did actually say that, but it didn't help him shake off the feeling that had come over him during luncheon — that in fact he was a fugitive Huguenot who had escaped during the St Bartholomew's Day Massacre, and that sitting to his left and right were his flayers, Mortier and Sanglier, whom he had conjured up in his imagination long ago.

Nor did these two men inspire trust in Nora Paskal, who,

43

moreover, had her own opinion of her husband's altruism. She said something to the effect that one of these days those beggars of his would rob them. Jan Paskal, however, was concerned about something quite different. He remembered the skin hidden in the wardrobe, the skin in which he had once felt too hot.

That time Diviš didn't make it to the pantry, so he never learned what had actually gone on there that Sunday, that All Souls' Day. For at that precise moment Mařenka Tůňka fell off the tree, and as he and Vojtěch raced downstairs, they collided with Pavel Santner who was carrying her up the stairs in his arms. When they all entered the pantry together and placed Mařenka Tůňka on the bed, all was in order as before. They didn't even overhear Grandmother Davidovič saying to Grandfather Davidovič: There, you see, he's come. She meant Pavel Santner. But what good was his coming when he had left Alice down there in the rain?

THE SOULS

We are the souls. We hover in the air. We live in fire and in water, we walk upon the Earth. Of all the elements, however, we prefer air, both the most abstract element, Anaximenes's *apeiron aer*, and at the same time the element most closely connected with life, with breath. We are breath personified, our inhalations and exhalations set the rhythm of the course of the universe. In the antinomy of life and death we are precisely on the boundary, on a boundary that is, alas, much too vague. We are half divine and half human, and this combination relates us to mythological heroes who descend to the earth to enlighten ignorant humankind.

We are endowed with a capacity for infinite metamorphoses and reincarnations that help us escape the prying eyes of mortals. They are everywhere around us, whether it be a Mr Sanglier or a Mr Mortier, or a Caretaker Briar in a mouse-grey overcoat. They are interested in things past, obscured long since by the dust of the pantry in which we like to abide. But most dangerous of all are the zealots like Diviš Paskal, who in their folly and dissolute curiosity overstep set limits. Should the dust be stirred up too much, we would be dispersed, for the greatest enemy of our integrity is entropy, or dissipation. Our defence is to cocoon ourselves in concrete things, in lasting and limited existence, we seek refuge in the element earth, awaiting the recurrence of conditions favourable to our return into the element air, for what is the purpose of our wings if not to fly? The closer we dwell to the ground, the greater looms the peril of our being swept up and dispersed, should we fail to be incarnate in an ephemeral human being or in a little animal who sleeps upside down in the pantry or frolics on the floor, or even just in someone's imagination, in a Paskalian phantasmagoria.

At every moment we are threatened by transition — pascha — pesach, by the transition from one phase into another, and to resist that transition is so tiring for us.

THE LIGHTWELL

How naïve, dear Diviš Paskal, to assume there exists a basic difference between a human being and an object, between the living and the dead, between a person and the world. One slips into the other very smoothly, and the moment and point of transition are imperceptible. Where, for example, is the boundary between the conch shell within and the world without that coils up and spirals back onto itself like a shell, as Teilhard de Chardin asserts? One has only to put one's ear to a seashell lying on some pantry shelf to hear the roar of the world. And in the same place where Diviš is listening to the world through the shell, Vojtěch, only yesterday, put his ear to Mařenka Tůňka's belly, seeming to hear the roaring sounds of his numerous descendants and of the descendants of their descendants.

Diviš has but to open the blind window to feel that through the lightwell he can hear the world, it comes in as the swish of wings fluttering and flapping as they crash against the walls of the narrow space. The world wafts in, roaring with the breath of those as yet unborn and with the posthumous breath of those long dead. Sometimes a bit of smoke from the furnace room mingles with the scent of the world, but Diviš breathes that in greedily, too. Eternal primeval night reigns in the lightwell. Only when Diviš looks up, when he leans far out and tilts his head sharply back, does he glimpse the shimmering little patch of light up high.

Diviš Paskal devises a way to step across the vent of the world. He constructs a passage from the pantry window to the bathroom window, repositioning and stretching a rope, and then, five floors high, he begins to cross over from one shore to the other. In the middle, where the rope sags lowest under his body's weight, is the world. At that point his body remains riveted. The crossing, which up to now was a downward journey, a descent with almost no bodily effort required, here appears equally demanding in either direction — it is a neckbreaking ascent. And then something unforeseen by Diviš Paskal occurs. His body must bear the total weight of the world and thus hasn't the strength to reach either of the windows through which it could re-enter the interior of the house, where weight again has only its usual, human dimensions. The body of Diviš Paskal, suspended spreadeagled in the lightwell, becomes, then and there, the world that will resound with a human voice, the world will scream for help through the mouth of Diviš Paskal.

Later on, as Diviš is hauled back with great difficulty into the pantry, for it is not yet granted to mortal Diviš to transcend the world — not even when it is only about four or five steps wide, a mere insignificant vent of a world as it exists in the lightwell of a block of flats — Diviš quietly moans, out of anxiety and shame.

Diviš's expedition into the world's lightwell alarmed the inhabitants of the pantry. Grandmother and Grandfather Davidovič stay up late into the night wondering whether they shouldn't, after all, leave their old home that is growing unsafe.

— Soon we won't even have the lightwell, isn't all the rest of the flat enough for them, grumbles Grandfather Davidovič. Grandmother Davidovič has to calm him down. Already earlier, Grandfather Davidovič had wanted to untie one end of the rope and let Diviš fall, but Grandmother Davidovič finally dissuaded him. — Now he is half ours anyway, she says. She too senses that Diviš Paskal's entry into the lightwell and his fleeting feeling of containing the world meant that from now on Diviš was halfway here and halfway already there, he would remain suspended spreadeagled between the two voids that would merge within him.

Diviš considers his expedition into the world a failure. Yet he already holds the world within himself, having inhaled it with the lightwell fumes mingled with a bit of smoke from the furnace room, because Caretaker Briar was just stoking the furnace. And when Diviš returns or rather is forced to return from the lightwell through the window, he'll see a girl in a dark dress with a white collar standing on the opposite sidewalk near the cemetery wall and she'll be gazing up at him. It occurs to him that this is probably Anna Domina whose wardrobe stands in their pantry, and that she has finally come back to claim it. He motions her to come up but she hesitates, as if she were not sure she was allowed, perhaps she has done something rash, perhaps she wanted like him to transcend the world and therefore now doesn't dare.

THE FLAYING

The fifties are unbearable years in the pantry. The lightwell is haunted by Herr Hergesell, he has come back, probably due to a nostalgic longing for the place where he lost his body. He keeps watch by the little window, patiently waiting for it to open and allow him to peek into the pantry. Grandfather and Grandmother Davidovič still command his respect, although from time to time he dares to shake his finger at them. A flock of curses from Grandfather Davidovič usually ensues, whereupon Herr Hergesell beats a humble retreat into more distant parts of the lightwell.

From time to time Alice Davidovič pays a visit to the pantry, but this happens quite rarely. She is always looking for her sweet-heart Pavel Santner and can't bear to stay in the pantry for long. Sometimes she brings along Diviš Paskal. By now the old folks have grown more accustomed to him, but when he first appeared, Grandfather Davidovič cried out: What does he want in here! And had Alice not been holding Diviš tightly by the hand, he would have slipped away from her and run off.

The wardrobe belonging to Anna Domina — to Alice Davidovič — still stands in the pantry. Of late, creaks and moans sound ever more often from its interior, and ominous cracks have appeared in its wood. The wardrobe speaks, even Jan Paskal can hear it when he is unable to fall asleep at night, and every now and then, when he is at home alone, he comes to see what is going on in the pantry. Jan Paskal walks around the wardrobe for a long time before finding the courage to open it after so many years. And immediately he sees: the skin has grown so much that it now fills all the space between the secular and clerical clothing, and several of its fungous pseudopodia have penetrated the chinks between the boards. Jan Paskal tries to estimate how much longer it will take for the skin to erupt from the wardrobe. He makes several attempts at pulling out the skin, always ripping off a piece and burning it in the middle of the pantry. But the skin doesn't ignite easily and then only smoulders. Before long the pantry is filled with smoke and Jan Paskal has to open the little window onto the lightwell.

Grandfather and Grandmother Davidovič are so completely blackened by the smoke that Alice is horrified when she comes in one day: My God, you look as if you'd been pulled through a chimney! Her words make Grandmother Davidovič remember something horrible from the past, probably the chimney in Poland, and she almost bursts into tears. Alice then has to spend a long time begging her forgiveness, she never intended to hurt her feelings, but Grandmother is touchy and overly sensitive and reproaches Alice for her callousness.

Some years after the war, pastor Paskal leaves the bosom of the Church of the Bohemian Brethren, he leaves it of his own free will. He is now outside the gates of paradise — in a street called the Garden of Paradise, in a shop dealing in feathers and skins of all kinds. Day after day, the former clergyman sinks his fingers into goose down and sheep fleece, he examines skins of rabbits, hares, cats, and various others. Countless times a day, in his imagination, he also touches the forbidden skin hypertrophying all the while in his pantry, the skin of a sin now seven years old. While running his fingers through sheep fleece, Jan Paskal reminisces about the sheep in the temple making way for Hergesell the wolf, about the sheep torn to pieces whose fleece covered the streets like snow. Why didn't he raise his fist already then, at the altar, in place of humility and obedience, he should have already then…. Under the delusion of abiding by the commandment *Thou shalt not kill*, he succumbed to cowardice. And even that he managed to explain away to his own advantage.

— Four rabbit skins, two goat skins. Jan Paskal puts the skins into a sack. He raised his fist only when he was about to be accused by the world: You howled with the wolf. Only then, but not even that time… — Two rabbit skins and one cat skin. Into the sack they go. In the Garden of Paradise Jan Paskal has plenty of time to ponder his life. — One wolf skin! Yet those words aren't uttered by Jan Paskal but by one of the two men he has seen before, by one of the two strange beggars he named after Catholic knaves from the St Bartholomew's Day Massacre. The man throws a skin on the counter — some skin! — It is Paskal's coat, singed at the edges, covered with brown spots of blood, the coat of the lamb who bit through the wolf's throat. And now the lamb is trembling in the tight grip of the two voids on either side who are taking him to the infamous Bartholomew Street.

See how well the skin fits the lamb! In it Jan Paskal feels himself on fire. He had kindled the fire himself and then, after it had gone out, had failed to notice the still smouldering embers on the inside. — Hercules wearing a skin steeped in the blood of the centaur Nessus. What price are you willing to pay, Puscall, so you can again cast off the skin stained with the centaur's blood? He should think it over well, they won't rush him. They leave him standing for hours on end, the skin pulled over his head. In Bartholomew Street, poor Jan Paskal signs his soul away to the devil in his double identity. Mortier and Sanglier sprinkle the pact with sand to prevent it from smudging.

It is they who let out death, the skin, and now it is doing its wretched work. Jan Paskal is put on the wheel. Or is it just the skin being broken on the wheel, the skin from the pantry about which even Diviš is beginning to suspect a thing or two? The skin is being racked, the skin is being broken on the wheel, the skin is coming apart at the seams, moaning. Once taken off, the poor little skin is humble and rubs against the flayer's legs. If it had lips, it would plant Bartholomew kisses on their feet. And what is Paskal to do, what is he to do when they even threaten to tell his inquisitive son?

But what can Diviš be thinking about all this, seeing his father obediently trotting along between those two men, having to listen to an account of what those two gentlemen, with whom his father has now become friends, had ordered him for dinner at the Little Bears, what can Diviš be thinking about all this? Ever more often, and for longer intervals, Diviš locks himself up in the pantry, ever more often he seeks out the company of Alice Davidovič and has long conversations with her.

THE SPIRIT OF HAGIBOR

In every space there are evil places and good places, places of damnation and places elect. And apart from these there also exist borderline places, ambiguous places vacillating between good and evil, where the former imperceptibly passes into the latter, becoming its antithesis. It is advisable to avoid such places, places where Paul turns into Saul, and Saul into Paul. These are dual places, places in both kinds. Such places, in fact, occupy most of existing space, while places clearly defined, homogeneous places, form mere islets of sorts, for places of transition are constantly growing in number, and even what is sharply defined keeps changing, only less abruptly and less obviously, hence its change can be observed only from a distance. Besides, the clear definition of places also tends to be weakened by general relativity, because what is a good place for one person or one thing, will be an evil place for another person or another thing, and vice versa. Thus, for example, not even the cemetery is an altogether evil place, for Mr Turk it was transformed into a vineyard, into a garden of delights, albeit briefly, and to the children the Olšany soil tasted of exotic fruit. And the house standing across from the cemetery is hardly an altogether good place, what with Caretaker Briar lurking at his little window, with mysterious crackling noises ever emanating from the pantry, and with Herr Hergesell haunting the lightwell.

And then it also happens that a place that has been a good place for a person at one time, becomes an evil place for him at another time, this is the most usual evolution of things. Besides that, there exists a close relationship between a place and a being called *genius loci*. The place passes into the being in a singular way.

Not far from Olšany is the mysterious Hagibor, a strip of wasteland named after the Jewish Home that stands at its edge. But it isn't just Hagibor, a Jewish meeting place and subsequently a German torture chamber, after the war, in the children's parlance it becomes Adderbor, or just Adder, undoubtedly referring to the serpents who guard the passages to the underworld. At once, through the exchange of a few letters, a place elect turns into a place of damnation.

And Hagibor-Adderbor is also a red wasteland, red with the sand of the tennis courts raked by Doe, a young man from Prague's Vršovice quarter. In his day, young Doctor Pelt used to play on one of those courts and young Doe from Vršovice would pick up his tennis balls. And later on Doe picks up the tennis balls for Nora Pelt, and after that for Vojtěch Paskal… no, Doe no longer picks up tennis balls for Vojtěch, no, not for him. By this time Doe is neither fast nor nimble enough any more, by this time Doe just hangs around, there behind the wire fence where the red tennis courts border on the wasteland thickly overgrown with bushes, where wild men kill little children. Doe — the spirit of Hagibor. Always nosing about in the bushes, descending into ravines, searching for lost tennis balls, lost so long ago. From time to time he does find a ball and carries it triumphantly along the tall wire fence to his hiding place. And sometimes Doe surprises lovers in the bushes, and sometimes even a wild man lurking there for little children.

At the height of the season, Doe spends long hours hanging around behind the fence. He dreams of the bygone days of the First Republic when, all in white, he would sprint after balls, dive after them with remarkable alacrity, climb up to retrieve them from the crowns of trees, crawl through thorny bushes. For, in those days, Doe was the best ball boy at Hagibor. Doe imagines that one day a ball will come flying over the wire fence and he will dive after it as before, everybody will admire his alacrity and he, Doe from Vršovice, will be called back to serve as a Hagibor ball boy once again, the best of them all. And then the First Republic, that time of paradise, will return as well.

However, when a ball does come flying over the fence, Doe is never fast enough, one of the children always beats him to it and throws it back, and all he has left are the ancient, shabby balls, no longer useful, some are already falling apart, maybe they arrived all the way from the First Republic — balls from paradise. Nonetheless, Doe keeps piling them up in a heap, by now he has a whole stash, balls from every period. What if the Golden Age returned one day, what if Doe's kingdom came, and all those shabby balls suddenly changed into brand new ones, into balls of the First Republic? And Doe, all in white, would pick them up and hand them to Doctor Pelt, and after him he would pick them up and hand them to Nora Paskal, and after her to Vojtěch Paskal, to him too, and after him…

Doe from Vršovice stands behind the tall wire fence that separates the red tennis courts from the wasteland, awaiting the arrival of the ball from paradise, the beginning of the mysterious metamorphosis. But meanwhile a cleaning crew headed by Caretaker Briar arrives in a truck, and to the tune 'It's me, me, the young freedom, the blossoming red flower, freedom young, abloom in red', they load up Doe's heap of balls, they haul away the First Republic.

Doe roams all over Hagibor searching for balls. He thinks someone has buried them and digs here and there in the ground. For if Doe doesn't find his tennis balls, those blessed times will never return, Doe, all in white, won't be the Hagibor ball boy. Nor will Doe's First Republic ever return.

THE BROTHERS SHMID

At the beginning of every summer, year after year, a ship lies at anchor near Olšany. Her two white masts sway in the wind, the brothers Shmid climb up and do handstands at the top. The view that always opens up before their eyes presents everything in reverse — the cemetery is up and the sky is down. There on the masts a different hierarchy rules and a different law of nature applies, turning everything topsy-turvy. The fee is three crowns for adults, one crown for children, and those who happen to have windows overlooking the square can see the show free of charge.

At the corner, by the black glass façade of the pharmacy, stands Georgie Briar, not daring to proceed. He thinks he has caught a glimpse of Alice Davidovič among the cluster of onlookers, her head tilted back, her eyes riveted on the tip of the mast.

Alice Davidovič really is there, Georgie is not mistaken, because Alice feels strongly attracted to this kind of spectacle, she feels a bond of kinship with those men on the masts. The world at Olšany has appeared to them as it has to no one else, in reverse perspective, all three of them have experienced the same flight, though in the case of the brothers Shmid it was rather a slide down the smooth body of the mast embraced by their arms. (One of them, Karel, did plunge to his death later on, but that happened somewhere else.) When the brothers Shmid do their handstands up so high, Alice feels the little Davidovič stir in her womb. And she covers her belly with her hands, as if trying to protect the child from the world and from Georgie's pin (after all Georgie is standing right there at the corner, by the pharmacy). She doesn't like that part of the programme where one of the acrobats slips lower and puts a rope between his teeth. The rope holds a motorcycle with the acrobat's children, dressed in sailor suits, sitting on it. As soon as they prepare for this act to begin, Alice walks around the square to avoid encountering Georgie Briar near the pharmacy — he hasn't changed a bit in all these years — and takes a detour home through Kouřim Street and Zásmuky Lane.

Georgie, unaware of Alice's ruse, keeps standing by the black glass façade of the pharmacy, his eyes searching for her. But in the spot where he caught sight of Alice a moment ago, there is only Diviš Paskal, standing now as if Alice had dissolved into him. Suddenly Georgie notices his own image in the glass façade. He is elated, for he has discovered something he had long considered lost, believing that his image had remained imprinted forever on the surface of Bubeník's soda counter. And Georgie, who has found his lost image, hops and skips happily on his way home. And as he approaches his house, he seems to see Alice's shadow disappear through the door. And since Georgie has just discovered his lost image and would like to tell Alice about it, he runs up after her to the fifth floor. — Where did you hide Georgie's Alice? he screams, after racing through the whole flat where the Paskals now live. — Where did you hide Georgie's Alice? He is still screaming as Caretaker Briar carries him downstairs, and he repeats the question, sobbing, as Caretaker Briar puts him on the sofa. For the sofa is the place that has been assigned in this world to Georgie, the eternal child. Had Georgie stayed on the sofa, he would never have seen Alice Davidovič through the little window onto the hallway, he would never have drunk Bubeník's water, the living water, he would never have held his hand inside Alice's muff. Had he not got up from the sofa, he would never have seen his own image, actually two images by now — one at the pub and the other in the black glass of the pharmacy. Those ill-fated outings (and here Alice is in part guilty too) gave rise to Georgie's love and hate, longing and self-love, jealousy and remorse, sadness and nostalgia. For had Georgie Briar never set forth from the sofa into the world, neither would he ever have risen against the world with a pin in hand.

And as Georgie whines on the sofa, one of the Shmid brothers is hanging upside down from the mast, holding a rope in his teeth from which dangles a motorcycle with children in sailor suits sitting on it. One of the children is Nanynka Shmid. The motorcycle spins like a top, Nanynka Shmid also spins like a top. Adults pay three crowns each, children one crown. And those as fortunate as Mr Hamza, whose windows open directly onto the square, can see the show absolutely free of charge.

Diviš Paskal is standing there mum, his eyes glued to Nanynka Shmid. When he runs into her the following morning, Nanynka is carrying a pitcher of milk from which she sips as she goes. And as Nanynka passes Diviš, the scent of distant shores and carousels at country fairs wafts over him and makes him dizzy. And the same scent wafts over Alice Davidovič who is standing nearby. It reminds her of the scent she smelled that day during the war when, as she flew downward, the world beneath her abruptly swayed, overturned and exuded an intense fragrance. — And those who happened to be walking by just then, such as Caretaker Briar, or Mr Turk and Mr Klečka who were on their way home from the Institute of Entomology, could see the show totally free of charge.

Jan Paskal, Paskal — the name sounds familiar to prosecutor Bark, but he can't remember where he came across it before. The case is a rather trivial one and essentially transparent. Some nasty business concerning a German, Hans Hergesell, a court clerk, whom pastor Paskal used to see during the war and whom, as the defendant Paskal has admitted, he killed for personal reasons. What these personal reasons were is easy to surmise. By a strange coincidence, the murder occurred on the eve of the outbreak of the anti-Nazi revolution of May 1945, which made it seem an act of heroism. But had it been a matter of heroism — Bark has his doubts about that — why would the defendant have left the church of his own volition and gone off to peddle rabbit skins? And why would he have tried in the pantry to burn his coat stained with the victim's blood?

To the question of why he attempted to destroy the blood-spattered coat, the defendant replies that he was convinced the coat was coming alive. At the time other symptoms of his illness began to emerge. — Of his illness? Bark raises doubts about that point. For example, Paskal was under the impression that someone was constantly tailing him and that someone was after his life. And there were two men and they apparently even threatened him with a wheel and a rack. And then they went beyond mere threats. When Bark presses the defendant to describe the persons who, as he claims, persecuted, threatened and tortured him, the former pastor pronounces two names: Mortier and Sanglier. There is laughter in the courtroom. The prosecutor points to the fact that the two names are obviously invented, unless, of course, they are the cover names of Western intelligence agents to whom Paskal was passing information. Information — about what? Apparently, Paskal really did make up those names, the two gentlemen never actually introduced themselves to him. Then he proceeds to babble something about a St Bartholomew's Day Massacre, about some ancestor of his, and the word skin crops up several times in his testimony.

At one moment during the trial Paskal suddenly jumps up and points to two decent-looking men seated in the courtroom: That's them, there they are, he shouts. It seems it was this very moment in the trial that led to the court's decision to acquit Paskal, despite Bark's attempts to prove that the defendant was merely feigning insanity. Be that as it may, it was impossible to prove Paskal's wartime collaboration, and the murder of a German in those heated days of historic events did not qualify as murder.

It is only outside, as he steps over a puddle that has formed in front of the courthouse entrance, that Bark remembers. There was a place called Babylon, a Babylonian confusion of tongues in a decrepit gazebo, it was winter of the first year after the war. He was making love to a woman married for less than a year, he had picked her up at Wilson station. Her name was something like that, she, too, was slightly raving, like the former pastor. She was talking about someone named Pelt, who had wronged her, but she was ready to forgive him everything. In the end, Pelt turned out to be her father. The memory of his postwar lovemaking makes Bark slightly dizzy. There in that gazebo, on the floor, there was also a lot of water.

PLAYING COPS AND ROBBERS

Diviš Paskal and Nanynka Shmid are hiding in a tomb. They are sitting on the ground behind an angel whose head is strangely tilted to the side, as though it might fall off at any moment. Nanynka Shmid smells of distant shores and country fairs, the carousel scent makes Diviš's head spin. Both are still out of breath from having run all the way from the house to the pharmacy, across the square, through Kouřim Street and down the narrow Zásmuky Lane, then climbing the wall and jumping. Their fingers sink into the soft soil, damp from recent rain. Then it occurs to them to hide in the tomb. Nanynka Shmid is a little afraid, she is also afraid of the strange angel (and what if she knew about Mr Turk inside the tomb, looking at them and saying to himself: Look who's come to see us, Nanynka Shmid who sits with her brother on the motorcycle every evening and spins like a top). But Diviš Paskal isn't afraid, not he, he even brags about the dead obeying him, when Nanynka is with him she has nothing to fear. Where does he get his self-confidence? Mr Turk wonders.

Nanynka Shmid huddles by the angel with the tilted head. — This angel must have something wrong with his spine, says Diviš Paskal. Nanynka is scared, which surprises Diviš Paskal: Nanynka, how come up there you're not afraid, not up there, but down here you're scared? But those are two completely different things — up there and down here, can't Diviš see that? Especially when down here some Briar is always lurking about (Mr Turk knows very well that Georgie is behind the wall). And when Nanynka's brother and another boy come running past, asking if by chance Diviš and Nanynka haven't come running this way, they happen to be playing Cops and Robbers (a game that has been played for ages here at Olšany), Georgie points his finger at the wall.

Indeed, it all happens just as Mr Turk has predicted. Georgie Briar climbs to the top of the wall and sits astride it, dangling his feet. He likes the view from up here, it's different from the one he has from the sofa, or even from the pharmacy, faced in black glass, altogether different. Yet what if the two down below aren't Nanynka Shmid and Diviš Paskal at all, what if they are Alice Davidovič and Pavel Santner who have assumed a disguise to keep Georgie from recognizing them?

THE GROSSGLOCKNER

My name is Horngoat. My name is Hoardgold. These aren't our only names. We seldom introduce ourselves, even more rarely by our real names. That way we give people a chance to make up various names and nicknames for us. They are welcome to address us by them. One crazy little pastor gave us French names, Mortier and Sanglier.

Our names are Horngoat and Hoardgold. We're sitting at the Little Bears tavern, we've got Puscall between us, he's working on his second supper now. Once again we're climbing the Grossglockner in the Hohe Tauern range, elevation 3,797 metres, this time Horngoat sets out from Heiligenblut, Hoardgold from Kals. Who will decide which climb was the more exhausting one? — You there, Puscall. — Puscall, you decide for us.

Jan Paskal puts down his napkin, after first wiping his lips with it. — The big bell is sounding the alarm. Those who turn around will be saved. Every time he finishes a meal, he gets an urge to preach. And out come all the goatish heresies he used to hear as a child.

The descent is worse than the ascent, we agree on that. One wrong step and you're in the ravine separating the Grossglockner from the Kleinglockner. During every supper at the Little Bears, Horngoat and Hoardgold, two former mountaineers, climb the Grossglockner. At the same time on their plates they lay siege to the Bastion of Tábor, their favourite dish. By the time they reach the top, their plates are almost empty and once more there gapes the ravine, the abyss into which they are supposed to descend (Puscall never fails to say 'Gehenna'), to lower themselves to Heiligenblut ('Holy Blood,' Puscall always adds, taking a sip of his Budvar beer). They had a girl down there, the sacristan's daughter, whose favours they shared. They called her Anemone and it was to her, into her Carinthian bed, into her Carinthian arms, that they were actually lowering themselves. The devil knows which of those descents was the more exhausting one. — Puscall, judge for yourself.

The third time they go there, just before the Second World War, Anemone is no longer serving beer, they say she no longer even goes to ring the bell for her father. Anemone has been married off. Horngoat and Hoardgold are sitting in Heiligenblut, they no longer go climbing. They feel as if their mountain, their

Grossglockner, has been married off too. Who'd feel like climbing up there with no Carinthian arms waiting down below, ready to make one's head spin?

— So they've married off our Anemone, Horngoat and Hoardgold say to one another. — To hell with the mountain. They stay down below playing backgammon.

From the Little Bears tavern it's just a stone's throw to Bartholomew Street, but the descent from a mountain is always more exhausting. Once again the ravine appears. You, Horngoat, feel a bit queasy, you, Hoardgold, a bit dizzy, but for a long time now it hasn't been because of Anemone, not because of her. Because of what, then?

THE STINKHORN

In the Bohemian Paradise there is a city of rocks that the children from the Red Pioneer camp near the village of Vyskeř have named Vertebra. It has two gates: the main gate, wide enough for a fancy parade to pass through, and another one, hidden and narrow — Death Pass. It's possible to crawl through Death Pass only in one direction, to the outside of the city. The city has its own castle Vertebra, a city hall, an executioner's house and execution site, a pillory, and a university (Charles University), it even has its own White Lady — Claudia Glaire, who walks on the ramparts, wrapped in a white sheet. — Watch your step, Claudia! Diviš the jester is hopping on one foot, furtively watching her.

Claudia the White Lady strides over the ramparts with her face shrouded, she moves along almost blindfolded, while Diviš the jester trembles with anxiety. And suddenly Diviš the jester sees two of the executioner's henchmen (only yesterday they were claiming to be students) — Randy and Slash, lurking on the ramparts. When Claudia reaches them, they grab her and carry her off. Claudia the White Lady cries for help but the city below is asleep. They carry her to the city hall where Mayor Och is already waiting. He wants to have the White Lady solely for his own pleasure, he will have her pour his wine and tie the laces of his trainers.

In the morning, when the city of Vertebra discovers its White Lady missing, Diviš the jester is dispatched to plead for her. — Your Honour the mayor, return Claudia the White Lady to the city of Vertebra! And Diviš the jester begins to turn somersaults before Och. — Let God's judgment decide. Diviš the jester shall crawl through Death Pass, but in the opposite direction. Diviš the jester grows pale, this task is beyond his power, but Claudia the White Lady fastens upon him her pleading gaze.

And now Diviš the jester is crawling into the hole, slithering on his belly in the fine sand, now he is midway, at the spot where the passage is narrowest and veers sharply upwards. — Diviš, come on out, the citizens are shouting. The jester's body arches in an effort to get through the bend in the rock, the sand of death penetrates all his pores and his eyes, his body grows deathly still, it can move neither forward nor backward. Diviš the jester moans quietly.

Diviš the jester is pulled out by his feet, shamefully whipped and put in the pillory. From there he can see as far as the city hall, where Claudia the White Lady is tying the laces of Och's worn trainers.

Diviš Paskal is expelled from the camp in the Bohemian Paradise for tickling Claudia Glaire's neck during the showing of the propaganda film, *The Silent Barricade*, about the anti-Nazi revolution of May 1945. And for purposely not removing the stinkhorn near the camp's entrance before Professor Nejedlý, the Minister of Education, was to pass through. Diviš was in charge of that very section of the route. Who will ever understand that Diviš felt sorry for the mushroom because it grew in the same spot year after year, because it had stunk in the same spot since time immemorial? Even in the darkest night he could find his way to the camp guided by its foul odour. Diviš Paskal is not pardoned even after reading the professor his poem, *The Ancient Prologue*, which opened with the line 'Day has fallen asleep and night has descended upon the deep forest.' And he is not pardoned even after the withered old professor has put two dumpling slices on Diviš's plate. The other two he puts on Och's plate and asks him to repeat his name. Professor Nejedlý is hard of hearing and just keeps nodding his head at everything.

Diviš Paskal has been expelled from the Bohemian Paradise, he is going home. He tries, for the last time, to capture the stench of the stinkhorn, now he can smell it again even though they had uprooted it. The mushroom has survived, but Claudia the White Lady is probably lost forever, tomorrow in the city of Vertebra she'll again tie Och's shoelaces. Diviš can still feel the fine sand of death falling into his eyes, his body held in the grip of the passage, imprisoned in it for good. — Diviš, dear jester, you were fatefully mistaken in trying to turn around the course of events, attempting to advance in the opposite direction, though turning everything around is a jester's privilege. This jester's custom is not appreciated in the Red Pioneer camp at Vyskeř.

Years later, a wiser Diviš Paskal is travelling through the Bohemian Paradise and makes a stop at Vyskeř. He can go almost blind-folded, led by the foul stench of the stinkhorn surviving forever in the place where the camp was razed to the ground years ago. And up there, in the rocky pass to the city of Vertebra, right at its centre, Diviš's body is still held captive. Having stiffened in the sand as if in the lava of Pompeii, it will remain there, just like the eternal stinkhorn that survives generation after generation of stinkhorns, like the primeval mushroom through which this universe regenerates itself.

MOTHER-OF-PEARL TREES

Lately Nora Paskal recalls her childhood more and more often. Her ears are filled with the roaring sound of the shells, supplied by Rie & Co. to Koudelka & Co., where they were made into mother-of-pearl buttons. When as a child she would fall asleep in her grandmother's house, she could hear at night how the shells on the ground floor murmured mysteriously and sometimes rattled strangely as they slid to the floor from heaps piled up by time and the world economic crisis. In those days Grandmother Koudelka would donate a great part of the supply to the charity over which she presided, to be distributed among poor children. The poor children would then engage in shell battles in the streets, and every now and then the shells would even clatter right below the windows of the former residence of the Counts of Thurn and Taxis, later the seat of Koudelka & Co.

One after another, fresh drifts of shells pile up in Nora Paskal's memory, heaps of shells supplied by Rie & Co. Grandmother Koudelka herself appears to her in a dress embellished from top to bottom with mother-of-pearl buttons, a dress she once wore to the charity ball. A huge shell adorns her tall coiffure, and as her grandmother bends down to Nora, it is not the sea that resounds, but Pardubice's stream, the Chrudimka. That day, at the charity ball, Grandmother Koudelka was solemnly pronounced the Mother-of-Pearl Queen. They say she even received an invitation to the castle from Baron Richard von Drasche, but since it was a fast day, nothing but buckwheat porridge was served.

Grandmother Koudelka, the erstwhile Mother-of-Pearl Queen, by then almost ninety years old, appeared one day in the flat across from the Olšany Cemetery. She was holding two flower pots in her hands. — I've planted some shells for you, she whispered in Nora Paskal's ear, they'll grow into little mother-of-pearl trees. But, Nora darling, don't forget to water them every day.

The flowerpots have been standing in the pantry ever since. The shell tubers have long since taken root in the soil of the pantry. Nora Paskal blows off a thin layer of dust. Grandmother Koudelka was right, little mother-of-pearl trees have sprouted up. A pity I haven't watered them, as Grandmother advised.

As soon as Nora Paskal sprinkles the little trees with water, she senses her grandmother's eyes looking out at her. That very moment a gush of water, the Chrudimka stream, bursts from the lightwell, soon the pantry is filled with water. And it is no longer a pantry in a block of flats across from the Olšany Cemetery but a gazebo at the foot of Babylon Mountain, first destroyed by the element fire, and now being destroyed by the element water. Nora Paskal takes off her dress, heavy with water, and with slow, circular motions washes off her soiled Babylonian belly. And then, in a corner of the gazebo, she catches sight of Bark, the law student, a current of water seizes him and carries him away. It is then that Nora Paskal remembers Pelt. How could she have forgotten about him? Pelt is still sitting in the white wicker chair as if rooted in the earth, or rather in the water, delivering his endless discourse on Skin, *de morbis cutaneis*, and naturally, as is just like him, he hasn't noticed the water seeping into his sparse ashen goatee. Nora wants to warn him, Pelt can't swim, but it's too late now, the water has poured over Pelt's head. And then the torrent sweeps up the gazebo itself and carries it all the way to the foot of Babylon Mountain, which from then on is washed by the waters of the Chrudimka stream. There it is cast up just as the waters of the flood cast up Noah's ark. When the water recedes, Nora Paskal finds a few boards from the gazebo on the mountain slope and puts them away in the pantry, beside her little trees. Their spindly, mother-of-pearl stalks are climbing toward the window of the lightwell, softly rattling in the draft.

Nora Paskal can spend hours upon hours sitting in the pantry, listening to the mysterious rattling. Grandfather and Grandmother Davidovič furtively watch her, shaking their heads: Look! She must have completely lost her mind, they tell each other. They already suspect a tumour the size of a shell is growing in Nora Paskal's head. That's why they also forgive her daily routine of pouring water all over the pantry. Mixed with the fine dust, the water produces slimy mud that makes Grandmother Davidovič's feet slip.

For three days now Diviš Paskal has been sitting in the pantry, grieving for his mother. Grandmother Davidovič feels rather sorry for him, she would like to console him, she would like to tell him that Nora Paskal is nearby, he has only to open the little window. But Grandfather Davidovič keeps an eye on her, he doesn't much like Diviš, he might even do something to harm him, should Grandmother disobey and speak kindly to Diviš. If Grandmother Davidovič had onions, she would make Diviš some onion soup, that soup would do him good. It has been so long since Pavel Santner brought the last onions. Now this one, it would never occur to him to bring onions, not even one. Grandmother Davidovič sighs. And Diviš Paskal hears that sigh and looks around in surprise.

Then later, when Diviš goes into the children's room, he sees Alice Davidovič sitting on his bed. She asks whether he has already found Pavel Santner. Again he has to disappoint her, he located only a Pavel Shantner and an Otto Santner, as if Pavel Santner had been swallowed up by the earth. He may also be dead by now. But Alice shakes her head. It's all right, she'll come another time, she's used to waiting. Even Grandmother Davidovič in the pantry waited many years for Grandfather to come back from Mrs Soška's, and he did come back and now he'll never leave her. Just as long as Pavel Santner isn't hiding from Alice, having no intention whatsoever to come and ask Grandfather Davidovič for her hand, just as long as he's not hiding. But if Diviš wants to do something for Alice, he should bring some onions, some ordinary onions, only he mustn't buy them nor receive them as a gift. Who knows, the onions might bring about the miracle of rebirth.

THE WEREWOLF

That which Diviš refers to as the spanning of two elements, earth and water, mountain and abyss, life and death, two motions — unwinding and rewinding, and which he considers to be his hallmark, Grandmother Davidovič in the pantry refers to with one word: werewolf. — Just take a look through the keyhole, she tells Alice, that's not a man but a beast — half sheep and half wolf, just take a good look. And pay no mind to all his talk about resurrection, dearie. One day he'll want to take you away from the pantry, but that'll be a ruse.

Alice doesn't quite believe Grandmother's words, what if Grandmother is just trying to turn her away from Diviš because she would be left alone with Grandfather, what if Grandmother doesn't want Alice to join Pavel Santner? After all, even that one time in the past she didn't want it, but Alice went ahead against her will. And suddenly a thought occurs to Alice: what if Grandmother and Grandfather deliberately didn't tell her that Pavel Santner had come by? And perhaps they made him believe that Alice had found someone else, Diviš, who's alive, and that's why Pavel Santner will never come back. And if Diviš Paskal is a werewolf, as Grandmother Davidovič now claims, though she rather liked him before, isn't it quite natural considering that a person is always caught between Heaven and Hell, living life in the middle, only the dead dwell up there — like angels, or down here — like beasts, or alternately up and down. Grandmother Davidovič is evidently prejudiced against Diviš the way the dead are prejudiced against the living, and besides, she can't forgive him for living in a flat that used to be theirs. But that is not Diviš's fault, that at least is not. And can one hold his having penetrated the world of the dead against him, when the dead themselves are trying so hard to penetrate the world of the living, trying, in fact, even to devour it and to instil their graveyard truths and laws everywhere?

Alice isn't quite sure whether she is making excuses for Diviš simply because she expects from him exactly what Grandmother Davidovič is trying to dissuade her from, because deep within her heart there is still a spark of hope for a new life. What if Mr Erben, the poet, is right when he occasionally proclaims at the Olšany Cemetery: That time will come, that day will be reborn, which makes dead branches sprout green leaves again. Then, in the splendour of that blessed morn, the dead will also rise to salute its reign.

Grandmother Davidovič suspects what is racing through Alice's mind. She too used to imagine things that way. She too used to hear Mr Erben prophesying on his grave, it was always in the springtime when the grass on the graves first turned green, except — as the saying goes — springtime grass lasts as long as it lasts. But Alice must find that out for herself, that's all there is to it.

One day Diviš realizes it was on the day they pulled him from the lightwell that he saw Alice for the very first time. He was covered with the lightwell dust, the dust was in his hair, it had gone into his nose, his ears and his eyes, particles of the lightwell universe, that realm of the dead, clung to him, and some remained even after he had bathed. And then, when he looked out of the window before going to sleep, he saw Alice standing down below. Since then Diviš has seen her waiting around several times, always looking up in his direction, and he has had the strange feeling of usurping her place.

He wonders why it is that, when his father enters the pantry, he finds no one there, neither Grandfather Davidovič nor Grandmother Davidovič, let alone Alice. She is very difficult to catch because she is almost continuously on the move between the house and Gallows Hill in the Žižkov quarter. Alice goes there to meet Pavel Santner, persuaded that should Pavel Santner return, his first steps would take him there, to the place where they used to go together on their way from school. But as soon as Alice reaches the very top where the gallows once stood and where now stands a semicircle of trees, their crowns battered into sugarloaf shapes by the wind, she is seized by the fear of missing Pavel Santner. What if Pavel Santner has gone to look for her at home and, not finding her there, has begun to grow suspicious? Under such circumstances it quite naturally would never occur to him to ask Grandfather Davidovič for her hand, he might even use it as a good excuse not to have to do so. So fragile was Alice Davidovič's certainty about Pavel Santner's love. And she hurried back from Gallows Hill, running along the Olšany pond and past St Roch's chapel, running even uphill alongside the cemetery wall until she was quite out of breath. But then again she was afraid of running into Pavel Santner halfway up the hill, or at the top, because he would see how quite out of breath she was from her rush to reach him, he wouldn't be pleased, he never liked to see her openly show her love for him. Should they run into each other right there, she mustn't let him notice she had been in such a hurry, and she'd quickly have to come up with a reason to explain why she was taking that route. To play it safe, she had a reason ready at all times and also tried to keep her breathing as even as possible, although it was now difficult because a new Davidovič was growing within her. But she never had to state the reason because she never ran into Pavel Santner. That's why Alice was always on the move and couldn't bear to stay in the pantry for long.

Diviš tried several times to dissuade Alice from making her trips, he lay in wait for her between the house and Gallows Hill, but Alice always passed without noticing him, she had eyes only for Pavel Santner, only for him. And Diviš's words never reached her.

Diviš Paskal begins to understand — the dead go on living among us, living their ordinary lives, lives strangely stark, as if reduced to what was essential to them, which after death is repeated over and over again. As if one got on a strange carousel from which there was no getting off, and one had to keep going round and round, spinning like a top. The dead go on living but we don't see them, we can only see them when we find ourselves in a state between life and death. These are Diviš's reflections. Diviš, however, considers himself an exceptional case, he feels he has been chosen to descend among the dead, to speak with them, and he is even convinced he could lead the souls out of their world, pluck them off their other-worldly carousel, naïvely thinking he would be doing them a favour, as if returning to this life were a pleasure.

Diviš wants to win over Alice Davidovič, he wants to lead

68

her out of the pantry, to interrupt her errant wanderings. And he thinks he will succeed by talking her out of her love for Pavel Santner. He begins to present Alice with reasons why Pavel Santner is bad and unworthy of her love. And one day Diviš says to Alice: Can't you see that Pavel Santner never really loved you, he stayed with you only out of pity. After those wicked words Alice turns away from Diviš and doesn't appear for a long time. But, most likely, Diviš is doing all this only because he is jealous of Pavel Santner and feels hatred for him despite the distance between them. That's the way it is, Diviš wants Alice for himself and he even entertains the thought of introducing her to his father. He wants to marry her, even though marrying a dead girl seems impossible, he wants to adopt Pavel Santner's child, the one Alice is carrying. But then Diviš has always had bizarre ideas and desired impossible things.

One summer day Diviš really does take the unsuspecting Alice by the hand when she happens to be at home for a moment, and leads her away from the pantry. But as they reach the door Grandmother Davidovič calls after them, saying that Alice has left her muff behind, and Diviš turns to look back. And as he looks back, Alice slips out of his grasp and runs away, once again she is running along her route to Žižkov. And then Diviš realizes that the muff was nothing but Grandmother's invention, he has never seen one in the pantry, and furthermore, why should Alice have to bring along a muff when it's summer and he's only taking her to meet his father. Grandmother Davidovič simply didn't want Diviš to take Alice away, they would feel lonely without her in the pantry, even lonelier than now, though she just comes and goes in a hurry. Who has ever heard of a living man marrying a dead girl, even though Alice is expecting a child and that child should have a father? What sort of happiness would this bring to all of them? It would be like in those fairytales where the youth marries a nymph and then, after breaking a rule, he is never to see her again, and they are both unhappy forever after and there is a curse on their children as well. Or the nymph leads the youth into a bog or into an abyss. But those who play with fire perish by fire. And having chosen Alice once and for all, Diviš must be prepared that she may lead him beneath the gallows on top of the hill or even to the cemetery. And he shouldn't be surprised if one day she forgets that Diviš, unlike her, cannot leave through the window.

Had Diviš seen through Grandmother's ruse with the muff and not turned to look back, he might have succeeded in leading Alice away from the pantry. But this way everything continues as before: Alice keeps going to meet Pavel Santner and rushing in to inquire whether Pavel Santner hasn't come by, and Diviš always sees her only for a moment, sometimes exchanging a few words with her. But Alice is impatient and as soon as she sees that Diviš has no news of Pavel Santner, she doesn't even let him finish and hurries away on her usual route. No, no, for nothing in the world will she allow Diviš to accompany her. What would Pavel Santner say if he saw them together? Today he is in France but in an instant he may be here in Žižkov, for in their temporality it is possible to get from one place to another instantaneously. But why then isn't Alice's journey any shorter than it would be, say, for Diviš, and why does walking uphill make Alice so short of breath?

Yet once again Alice is no longer listening to Diviš, she's covering her ears, Alice knows that Diviš is trying to turn her away from Pavel Santner, that he wants her to accept his misgivings, which in time would dissolve even the strongest emotion. Diviš doesn't understand that Alice makes a point of not shortening her journeys, of course she could fly effortlessly straight from the window to the top of the hill, she wouldn't even have to fly there at all because she knows only too well that Pavel Santner isn't there yet, and won't be there for some time. Alice must first wear out seven pairs of shoes before she can see her sweetheart again, before Pavel Santner, travelling on business along the Côte d'Azur, arrives in Èze, an eagle's nest of a little town, from where he'll come straight to Gallows Hill.

But what can Diviš Paskal know about all this? He wants

to save Alice, to deprive her of her fate, yet at the same time is incapable of stopping himself from looking back as he leads her out of the pantry, spoiling it all for the sake of a muff lost long ago. When Alice jumped out of her window, she hid her hands in it because she was afraid of the world, but as she flew, her hands reached up over her head like the hands of someone drowning reach up for the water's surface. The muff flew off somewhere to the side and someone picked it up, probably never imagining it belonged to the dead girl whose face was growing sodden with wet snow. That's how it happened, but perhaps it happened somewhat differently. Where was Diviš the saviour then, why didn't he come rushing to her, why didn't he catch her hands and pick up the muff, why did he deliver Alice, muff and all, into the arms of the world and of death from whose embrace he was now trying to wrestle her? But how could Diviš have been there, when he hadn't even been born yet?

THE MUFF

I am a muff, a Persian lamb muff. My pelt is from Persian lambs as yet unborn. My fur is genuine, it's no imitation, no krimmer. My coat is shiny, and one can sink one's fingertips deep into its folds. Pavel Santner felt the luscious softness once during the war, before he left with a transport, when he held me in his hand, perhaps thinking of Alice Davidovič's soft lap.

I am a muff, a little grotto for lambs who seek shelter inside me, for Alice Davidovič's hands, which hide inside me from the world of wolves. But then the world suddenly breaks in two under the weight of a human body falling at free-fall speed, and the hands abandon my hiding place, trusting that someone will catch them and ease their fall. I'm flying through the air at a slower pace than the body, I'm still gliding to the ground after the body has taken up its final position on the sidewalk. Who knows, maybe if Alice Davidovič hadn't dropped me, she would have descended together with me, she would have flown down not like a black lamb but like a black bird.

My shiny, soft fur is drenched with wet snow. I'm lying in the road, not far from the cemetery wall. Just a bit more and I would have made it over. Doe from Vršovice, the one who used to pick up balls at Hagibor, passes by, his eyes scrutinize me, but since I'm not what Doe is looking for, he goes on. And here comes Caretaker Briar. See here, a muff. The dead girl can't be helped any more but why waste the muff, it's nice, it's Persian lamb. And now Mr Turk and Mr Klečka come hurrying by, just on their way home from the Institute of Entomology, now they're bending over Alice, Mr Klečka would like to put the muff under her head, but where has it gone? Mr Turk saw Caretaker Briar stuffing the muff under his caretaker's coat. Of what use is it to him when he has only Georgie? Why, is Georgie about to sit on the sofa with his hands in the muff? And Mr Turk says to Mr Klečka: How shabby! And he says it loud enough for Caretaker Briar to overhear as he hurries home, the front of his mouse-grey coat oddly bulging.

In the evening Mr Turk and Mr Klečka are having supper together, as usual without much appetite. Once more they're discussing how the accident occurred and how Caretaker Briar stole the muff and carried it off under his coat, and how Mr Turk said How shabby! on purpose loud enough for Caretaker Briar to overhear. Mr Klečka quite agrees with what Mr Turk said, he's just a little worried that Caretaker Briar may get back at Mr Turk for this one day, he's obviously hand in glove with the Germans. And they also talk about Pavel Santner, it's been several days since he left with a transport. — Such a good-looking young man, Mr Klečka says. And tomorrow it'll be the Davidovičes, actually only Herta Davidovič, Alice won't be going any more, and neither will Grandfather Davidovič. Once in a while somebody does return from Hagibor, but from a camp — who knows? Pavel Santner left several days ago, Herta Davidovič is leaving tomorrow, and the day after tomorrow — Mr Klečka doesn't want Mr Turk to finish. But Mr Turk knows he can't keep hiding behind his Turkish name. And where else could he hide and not leave Mr Klečka all alone? And that's when Mr Turk gets the idea of hiding in the cemetery, that way Mr Klečka won't have far to go, and maybe the war will be over soon.

And while Mr Turk and Mr Klečka are talking at home for the last time, Caretaker Briar goes to make sure the muff is in its place — in a cabinet where he also keeps his record book. Caretaker Briar reaches inside, the muff is there, Caretaker Briar sinks his fingers into the Persian lamb fur, the curls are still damp. Oh, if only Georgie Briar knew what a treasure his father was hiding from him! If Georgie found the muff, he could slip his arms into it up to his elbows, never again would he have to beg stingy Alice. But Georgie suspects nothing, and in the morning, when Caretaker Briar goes to buy his paper from Thomas Hamza, he takes the muff along. The muff is still damp as Caretaker Briar puts it on the counter. Thomas Hamza examines the muff — the muff is nice, of Persian lamb, but where has he seen it before? Of course, now he remembers, Herta Davidovič used to have one just like it, Thomas Hamza recognizes the muff, but it might very well be an altogether different one. He touches the muff with one finger, as though touching Christ's wound. If only Caretaker Briar isn't trying to trick him, if only this isn't some imitation, some krimmer. But it isn't krimmer, now Thomas Hamza has seen for himself, it's real Persian lamb, as black a lamb as they come. And as he sees Mr Vinkler entering his shop, he shoves it under the counter just to be safe, what if it's a stolen lamb, after all.

Thomas Hamza becomes ever more sure that it is Herta Davidovič's muff, he remembers it very well, Herta Davidovič always placed it on the counter and pulled her small hands out of it. Thomas Hamza always felt as if it was slightly indecent, as if it was not a matter of her hands but of something else. And one day Thomas Hamza couldn't help himself and kissed the small hands, one after the other, and his cheek brushed against the Persian lamb muff, it was damp then just like it is now, from the wet snow falling outside. — A beautiful little muff, Mr Köck.

Won't you buy it for your darling daughter? Mr Köck does buy it, why not, it really is a nice muff, Persian lamb.

I am Herta Davidovič's muff, she has grown old and become Grandmother Davidovič. She's the one who gave me to Alice so she could hide inside me from the world of wolves. I am Caretaker Briar's muff. I am the muff of Thomas Hamza, the tobacconist. I am the muff of Mr Köck from Kouřim Street, I am the muff of his darling daughter. At this moment she is walking hand in hand with young Thomas Hamza, those two are getting married soon. I feel Miss Köck's hand inside me.

Georgie Briar happens to be by the window, watching for Alice because he hasn't seen her for several days. He recognizes Alice Davidovič's muff at once, the muff of whose pleasure he has been deprived, he runs out and snatches the muff away from Mr Köck's darling daughter. — That's Alice Davidovič's muff, he shouts in her face. And he runs off with the muff to his sofa. Now Alice must come, he says to himself, now she must, she'll come for her muff. But Georgie won't give it to her right away, he'll tease Alice a bit, so she knows how it feels to have to beg someone all the time. And Georgie sits waiting on the sofa. He hides the muff inside the sofa, among the coiled springs, Father would surely rush to the fifth floor with it right away, and then Alice would never come down. Georgie waits and waits, but Alice doesn't come even then.

Every time Georgie Briar is at home alone, he is seized by temptation: What if he were to take out the muff and slip one, or both, of his hands inside. But without Alice, without her permission, it seems a sin to him. Year after year Georgie keeps sitting on the sofa. Down below him sleeps the muff. He could take the muff out and do it at any time. But he never does. And one day, many years later, Diviš Paskal appears on the sofa next to Georgie, he sits down in the very spot where Alice used to sit with Georgie, and something about him even resembles her slightly. Who knows if it isn't really Alice, Georgie suddenly thinks. And in the end Diviš succeeds in wheedling Georgie's muff secret out of him. In return, he promises to bring him Alice. But why on earth does he promise that to Georgie, knowing he has failed once before? Surely he doesn't think that one can make Georgie Briar, cursed into the form of an eternal child, believe anything? Georgie gives the muff to Diviš in exchange for his promise, he gives up the muff to get Alice back from Diviš. And Diviš carries the muff triumphantly to the pantry: Diviš Paskal can do the impossible.

Grandmother Davidovič examines the muff with mistrust, Alice is out again of course. — Is it really that muff, the muff she had since her youth, the same muff Alice took with her on her last journey, but then what became of it?

I am a muff, the Persian lamb fleece Diviš Paskal wheedled out of Georgie Briar and thus, having completed the circle of my errant wanderings — from the house to the cemetery, to the house, to the tobacconist's, to Kouřim Street, and into Georgie's sofa, I've returned to the place from which I set out into the world. And when Alice Davidovič takes me in her hand here in the pantry, she'll quickly cheer up a bit, for if her lost muff has returned to her, so will Pavel Santner return, it won't be long now till she goes out to meet him for the last time.

Meanwhile, the deceived one sits wailing on the sofa: Give Georgie back the muff! He had it here, quite nearby, just beneath him, all he needed to do…. He had the muff and now no longer has it. And Georgie Briar discovers the meanness of the world and feels the bitter transience of his things.

PASCHAL LAUGHTER

Every space faces life with one of its sides and death with the other, and the place of passage between the two cannot be determined with any certainty. Even a block of flats is not above this law. This one's front faces the Olšany Cemetery, its back blends into a tangle of houses and courtyards serving as a stage for children's wild games. If the foundation of the house were bared, speculates

Diviš Paskal, one would see that the roots of the house reach across the street, beyond the cemetery wall, all the way beneath the tombs of the German families, all the way beneath the tombs of the 19th-century nationalists. In front of one such tomb stands the melancholy angel. He used to prop his head on his hand the way Diviš Paskal is doing now.

Every space has its Promised Land and its underworld, just as a flat has a kitchen and a pantry wherein the rite of passage, that torture of body and soul, takes place. The youth is surrounded by the shadows of the dead who used to live there, he is among them and speaks with them. He is in a space that spirals back onto itself like a shell.

The father sits facing the son, the younger one who remains after the older one has rebelled. With a curious movement of his head, decrepit old Paskal reveals now and then that his neck was at one time constricted by a clerical collar. A clerical collar? Aren't those worn exclusively by Catholic priests, exclusively by the papists? Maybe it left behind an imperceptible groove now vanishing in the web of his wrinkles. His hands, smelling of various kinds of pelts, rest on his knees like two tanned skins — maybe rabbit skins he himself took to the market. To the Bartholomew Street market. From time to time the skins twitch nervously, as if the two little skinned animals have come back to life for a moment.

— And Father, what was the story with that German? Diviš doesn't say he sometimes hears the German haunting the lightwell, it happens on those anniversary days in May. (Then Grandmother Davidovič doesn't dare to crack open the little window even for a moment. — To hell with eternity, Grandfather Davidovič blasphemes. — Could it already be May again? Grandmother Davidovič wonders. And just to be safe, she keeps checking to make sure the little window is properly shut.) But it's only Easter, a time of dark memories and dark allusions for the two Paskals, a time of the lamb and the wolf, a night of transition full of strange tattered rags and skins like the pantry, that forbidden chamber of sin and chamber of initiation rites. But Easter is also a time of paschal laughter — *risus paschalis*, a time that allows everything sacred and everything deadly serious to be defiled, disparaged, and scorned with impunity.

Father Paskal laughs at his own tales with a laughter Diviš finds strikingly similar to the wry laughter of Grandfather Davidovič. And as Diviš looks at his father, he notices there is only a scrawny smidgen of paschal skin left of him, like the rag doll Death, burned to symbolize the end of winter, and he sees it shrivelling up day by day. He feels sorry for his father. And suddenly he can't stop himself from telling his father about Grandfather and Grandmother Davidovič who live in their pantry, and about the ridiculous Hergesell who haunts the lightwell. And he also tells him about Alice Davidovič and her child.

When Diviš utters Pavel Santner's name, Father seizes his hand. That name is familiar to him, perhaps he heard it mentioned in Bartholomew Street, so many names turned up there. Yes, they claimed the man had been to see him twice in the flat but is now abroad. But he had never laid eyes on the man, not ever, believe me, Mr Mortier and Mr Sanglier. Still how did Diviš happen upon this name, and how did he happen upon all the others, when they are names of people living and dead whom he could not know? Only now is Jan Paskal beginning to know his younger son, the one who at the age of twelve dropped himself down into the lightwell and now claims to see the dead and consort with them.

Jan Paskal takes his hands off his knees, as if trying to hold Diviš back. The skinned little animals have come back to life again, Diviš thinks. And at that moment he realizes his transgression, he should have remained silent, as Alice advised him. He has betrayed the souls, he has put them at the mercy of a living man who tomorrow will hurry with them to the market — to the Bartholomew Street market.

Alice Davidovič is wandering through the city in search of her sweetheart. She wants to confide her secret to him, even though she isn't too sure he'll be pleased to hear it. For several years now she has been carrying that secret within her, she has even kept it from Grandmother Davidovič, who often scrutinizes Alice's figure from head to toe. But of course Grandmother has known it for a long time. Soon Alice's time will come and then it will no longer be possible to hide anything. If Pavel Santner hasn't come by then to ask Grandfather Davidovič for her hand, Alice will be lost.

But how can Pavel Santner suspect that a life once conceived can come to term even within one who is dead? Pavel Santner came out of Bohemia as the children of Israel came out of Egypt, he crossed the wilderness by the Red Sea. Such was his passage. And now Pavel Santner is in Vienna, he got himself a position with Rie & Co., who are still in the shell business, married another girl long since and has two children with her. How lucky he turned up the collar of his winter coat on that All Souls' Day so Alice couldn't put her arms around his neck. Although in all likelihood had Pavel Santner found Alice after the war, he probably would have married her because, in his own way, he did love her. He did the most he could, he came looking for Alice twice but never found her at home, the first time he found a dead man with a slit throat in the pantry, the second time he brought in Mařenka Tůňka who had fallen off a tree. (She too is expecting at the time and miscarries a bastard that night. She names him František and puts the little corpse in a shoebox. Then Nora Paskal takes Mařenka Tůňka back to the village of Karhule below Blaník Mountain and banishes Son Vojtěch from the house. Father Paskal says nothing. And Vojtěch Paskal doesn't see this as punishment but as an injustice committed by a stepmother against a stepson. He is convinced that Diviš, in his place, would have been forgiven. Vojtěch tends to forget that Nora Paskal divided everything among the two sons into equal shares, shares that were perhaps too equal.

Vojtěch Paskal crosses his wilderness grumbling. He curses his home and swears never to set foot in it again.)

Pavel Santner is strolling along the seashore strewn with mounds of shells. He watches the dark hands of the half-naked natives swiftly sort the shells and throw the useless ones back into the sea. Their mother-of-pearl hues shimmer on the surface as the shells softly rattle. Pavel Santner bends down and sorts through them with the tenderness of a lover. Grains of salt cling to his hands. Blinded by the sun reflected from the shells, Pavel Santner squints with his nearsighted eyes.

At that moment Alice Davidovič feels her first labour pains. With her last ounce of strength she climbs to the fifth floor of the house opposite the Olšany Cemetery. In her belly she hears the murmur of a new Davidovič destined to be born in Egyptian captivity. — Grandmother!

Meanwhile Diviš Paskal is hurrying to the market in Havel Street. There he steals a bunch of onions and runs away. They run after him, now they've caught up with him, now they've got him, now they're taking him to Bartholomew Street. They've torn the bunch of onions from him, yet Diviš clutches one onion firmly in his hand — the onion that is to deliver a new Davidovič into the world. It will happen soon, perhaps any moment now, his cry will echo through the pantry, and Grandfather and Grandmother Davidovič will bend over the little child.

But who at the Bartholomew Street headquarters is ready to believe such tall tales? Not Major Bartošek. Little thief Paskal is led through endless rooms, in one of them he sees a man with his coat pulled over his head and a knave standing on either side. What does it matter that the onion will cost Diviš dearly, that it means the end of his ethnographic studies, when Diviš has discovered a new tribe inhabiting the world, or rather the pantry of a flat in a house across from the Olšany Cemetery. Right now a new descendant is being born there.

Look at him, he did it after all. Grandmother Davidovič examines the onion for a long time, turning it this way and that, as if not believing her eyes. She then hands the onion to Grandfather in the corner to peel. And this time Grandfather Davidovič doesn't drive Diviš Paskal away, he only mutters something under his breath. — It's just like the ones Pavel Santner brought, the same ones I used to make onion soup for Alice, but she never touched it, she was in such a hurry to go and meet Pavel Santner.

The bird sleeping upside down near the ceiling suddenly wakes up, flaps its wings, circles around and settles on Grandmother Davidovič's shoulder. — Look at that, the smell even woke up our greedy Chamberlain.

Grandmother, where is Alice? Diviš asks. — And where is the baby?

Grandmother Davidovič shakes her head over Diviš's lack of understanding. — She went to show the baby to Pavel Santner, naturally.

— But Pavel Sant… — Shhh, Grandmother Davidovič puts a finger to her lips.

GEORGIE BRIAR'S NOSTALGIA

Caretaker Briar guards the entrance to the house as if it were the entrance to the underworld. He guards it from arsonists who in these turbulent times start fires in cellars. — The class enemy is still at large, says Caretaker Briar, and keeps his eye especially on Paskal from the fifth floor. If he weren't a suspect, those two men wouldn't be coming to see him, wouldn't be asking about him. A Mr Horngoat and a Mr Hoardgold, he noticed them long ago. Now they're sitting on the sofa in Caretaker Briar's flat that reeks of yesterday's cabbage, Georgie Briar, cursed into the form of an eternal child, sits enthroned between them. Horngoat feeds Georgie white chocolate and Georgie calls him Kostya. Caretaker Briar hastily explains that Georgie is mistaking him for a Russian soldier, and from somewhere he produces the record book with the memorable entry. Next to that page there is inserted a post-card from the Caucasus showing Mount Salavat-dag, elevation 3,642 metres, from where Kostya Sukhoruchkov sends greetings to Caretaker Briar and his son Georgie.

Horngoat and Hoardgold carefully examine both the record book entry and the greetings, their eyes lingering especially long on the picture of Mount Salavat-dag, elevation 3,642 metres. After climbing the mountain with their eyes, for they are former mountaineers, they descend again, back to the sagging sofa and to Georgie, upon whom they bestow another portion of white chocolate. Caretaker Briar tells them how in 1945 he dragged the body of a dead German downstairs, a certain Hergesell, a court clerk, and how he then deposited it by the cemetery wall. It was a job for the plague knaves, the body was already decomposing. Horngoat listens to him and Hoardgold, his aide, takes down every word. The momentary nostalgia that overcame them at the sight of Mount Salavat-dag, and at the memory of Anemone, has already passed.

All of a sudden Georgie Briar abruptly gets up, making the two men on the sofa jump, and runs to the little window that opens onto the hallway. Georgie seems to recognize Alice's footsteps. It's winter again and Georgie would like to hide his hand in Alice's muff, this time he wouldn't stab her with a pin, not this time. But there's no one in the hallway, that's to say Alice isn't there, it's only Diviš Paskal passing by. Alice is probably hiding from Georgie because of the pin, most likely she doesn't want to forgive him, for Georgie hasn't seen her since that day. And her muff is also on his mind, where has it gone? Pavel Santner probably took it away and Alice was hiding in it. That's why Georgie didn't see her leave the house.

Georgie Briar shuffles back from the window to the sofa. He is thinking: when summer comes, maybe Alice will stop being angry and will take Georgie to Bubeník's pub, Georgie would so much like to drink again the miraculous water that burns his throat, he would so much like to observe his image in the shiny counter top.

What could have become of Alice Davidovič's muff? And where have Bubeník, his miraculous water and his shiny counter gone in these strange times? Georgie Briar feels the bitter transience of things first-hand, although he's enthroned in the middle of the stationary kingdom of the sofa, and precisely for that reason. Horngoat is stuffing white chocolate into Georgie's mouth and all of a sudden pulls back. A thorn of some kind has stabbed his hand, a thorn. He shouldn't have denied being Kostya Sukhoruchkov.

THE PASS NEAR THE BOTIČ STREAM

Diviš Paskal has glimpsed Claudia only once since he was put in the pillory, since the time he tickled her neck during the showing of the propaganda film, *The Silent Barricade*. He caught a glimpse of her one summer from a train between Čerčany and Mrač, standing behind a lowered barrier at a level crossing. Claudia was pressing to her body two aestival loaves of bread. Diviš calls out to Claudia from the train: The flour will make you all white, Claudia. That's just like Diviš, calling out something like that, all he can do is caution and warn people. But Claudia smiles at Diviš just the same. On the other side of the crossing, however, out of Diviš's sight, two knaves, Randy and Slash, are waiting for Claudia's loaves. And after the train has passed and Claudia hands them the loaves, she sees that Diviš was right, she's covered in flour and permits those two, Randy and Slash, to dust her off.

In the autumn, as the days grow shorter, Claudia begins to pine for Mrač where she won't return before another year has passed. She begins to feel uneasy in the company of Randy and Slash, who are constantly at her heels, she remembers Mayor Och and also Diviš the jester, and how he tried to defy Och's will. What if they were to build another city of Vertebra here in Prague's Nusle quarter, what does it matter that they are no longer children. Randy and Slash are game for anything. Even now the Nusle flat is being transformed into the city of Vertebra. The bathroom becomes the hangman's house, the toilet the pillory, and the space between two art nouveau wardrobes — Death Pass.

As Claudia the White Lady, wrapped in a bed sheet, walks on top of the wardrobes, Diviš calls to her: Watch your step, Claudia! Mayor Och sits in the kitchen waiting for the hangman's henchmen, Randy and Slash, to bring him the White Lady, because he has no one to pour his wine and tie his shoelaces. The knaves have already seized her from behind, the sheet slips off her shoulders, for an instant Diviš beholds Claudia's white body. Now the knaves carry Claudia to Mayor Och, now Claudia pours wine for Och and ties his shoelaces, the sheet continually slipping off her shoulders, now Diviš turns somersaults before Och, now he pleads for Claudia: Return Claudia the White Lady to the city of Vertebra (She really is white, Diviš thinks, as if the sun of Mrač had never even touched her)! Now Diviš squeezes between the two art nouveau wardrobes and gets caught, now Diviš is pulled out by his feet, shamefully whipped and set in the toilet bowl pillory.

And after the Nusle wine has gone to Mayor Och's head, he remembers the slightly deaf old geezer Nejedlý, and the two slices of dumpling still stuck in his throat. Diviš again has to recite the poem *The Ancient Prologue*, Nejedlý-Och nods his head, behind him stand his bodyguards, the knaves Randy and Slash. Nejedlý-Och pulls the sheet off Claudia, now Claudia stands there naked. But Claudia is already wrapping the sheet around herself like a toga. Suddenly the kitchen becomes Mount Olympus. And all white Claudia keeps refilling everyone's glasses. Overcome by the Nusle wine, Randy and Slash manage to crawl all the way into the hangman's house and fall asleep in the bathtub, Och-Zeus lays down his head under the Olympian table.

White Claudia wanders about the city of Vertebra but haunts only Diviš the jester, who lies in wait for her in the pass between the two wardrobes. He says to her: Claudia, you're all white. — It's from the loaves of bread, Claudia replies, allowing Diviš to dust her off. Claudia's hair falls into Diviš's eyes and mouth, he feels so tightly gripped within the pass that his head spins. At that

moment the volcano Petřín, towering over Prague, spews forth
lava that slowly engulfs the Nusle valley.

The hangman's knaves, Randy and Slash, sober up toward
morning, climb out of the bathtub and set forth to discover
Pompeii. Diviš gets a shameful flogging and is expelled from the
Nusle paradise. Before daybreak Diviš Paskal strides along the
foul-smelling Botič stream, and as he crosses the bridge he remembers the mushroom from Paradise. It's growing there somewhere,
still, and Diviš's body is still imprisoned in the pass — between
the two art nouveau wardrobes, in the lap of Claudia Glaire.

GALLOWS HILL

I am Benjamin, the youngest of the Davidovič line. I am the
voice calling in the pantry. Chamberlain the bird is breathing in
my face, Chambermaid the rat rubs against my legs, and, above
me, Hergesell's ghost descends through the lightwell and comes
after me. I live on onions and breadcrumbs. I am the one who
speaks in parables. Behold the naked ground from which a vine
sprouts overnight and bears grapes within the hour. I am life born
of death, life conceived in the womb of a dead girl. She rocks me
in the Sabbath tablecloth, singing softly.

Hergesell is in the lightwell, he has ordered the massacre of
all the innocent ones in the house. Alice, however, doesn't know
about this, she isn't contemplating a flight to Egypt, she's only
thinking of going to Žižkov to join Pavel Santner. Alice walks
downhill alongside the cemetery, she passes St Roch's chapel and
the Olšany pond, she comes to the house that stands at the foot of
Gallows Hill. Alice knows: Pavel Santner is not at home, not yet,
and so she goes to wait for him at the top of the hill where now
stands a semicircle of trees, their crowns battered into sugarloaf
shapes by the Žižkov wind. This was their chosen place, in the
sparse grass, among dog faeces. Alice places Benjamin in the centre
of the semicircle and immediately the trees close in around the

child to protect him from the Žižkov wind and inclement weather. But will they protect him from Hergesell the wolf, from Hergesell the eagle circling above their sugarloaf-shaped crowns?

Pavel Santner is in Èze, an eagle's nest of a little town. He climbs up a steep, winding street to the town's highest point. High up, a number of little streets converge into the Grande Corniche, a path above an abyss into which the town stares impassively. All along the way Pavel Santner is buying earthenware, his arms are full by the time he reaches the Grande Corniche and the Hotel Terminus — the End. End of what? End of the city on the rock, or of Pavel Santner, the shell merchant? And you shall shatter like a potter's vessel...

Pavel Santner doesn't look into the abyss, it's enough for him to look at the bottom of the earthenware jug he's balancing on his knees as he sits for a moment in the little rose garden overlooking the abyss. He puts the jug to his ear and in it seems to hear the wind whistling on top of Gallows Hill. The rose garden around him is suddenly full of dog faeces. Pavel Santner quickly gets up, and clasping the jug with the Žižkov wind and all the other earthenware pottery in his arms, he passes by the Hotel Terminus (end of what?) and hastily descends along a steep, winding alley all the way to the bottom of the abyss. Suddenly he has grown restless here, hastily he gets into his car, places the jug with the sound of the wind on the seat next to him, feels the wind slowly escaping from the jug, feels it swirling above his head, slowly turning it into the shape of the tree crowns atop Gallows Hill.

And now an oncoming dairy truck pushes Pavel Santner's car off the road, not into the abyss, just into the ditch, where it bursts into flames. And now Pavel Santner is walking along the path by the Žižkov percussion cap factory toward the top of Gallows Hill. The wind has shifted and Pavel Santner feels it at his back. The wind has shattered the potter's vessel in which it had been imprisoned and has swept him up along with itself to go home. And now the wind is back, swirling above the trees standing in a semicircle atop the hill, their crowns battered into the likeness of sugarloaves — and there, amidst them, stands Alice Davidovič.

Now they're running towards each other, now they've met, now Pavel Santner and Alice Davidovič are sitting together in the sparse grass in their chosen place, in Žižkov's little garden of delights, while Benjamin, left to his fate, is carried off by Hergesell, the eagle. And when those two finally look deep into each other's eyes, they realize how old they've grown. Pavel Santner sees that Alice is as ugly as her grandmother, and Alice Davidovič can tell from Pavel's tender caresses that other women have come between them. Pavel Santner's embrace doesn't hold her as tightly as it did before, it is weary and limp and will bring forth no new Davidovič.

Alice pulls away from Pavel Santner and looks around for the child, only now does she remember him, only now. She looks for the youngest of the Davidovič line to show Pavel Santner but doesn't find him. And Pavel Santner calls Alice an unfit mother and stifles her with reproaches. Maybe there never even was a child, and how could there ever have been one when Pavel Santner never got so far as to make it possible for Alice to conceive. And Pavel Santner calls Benjamin a mere fabrication on Alice's part by which she's trying to tie him down. And he says this because the source of his love has dried up, and also because he regrets the life that vanished after the car accident in the ditch near the little town of Èze in southern France. Pavel Santner gets up and dusts blades of grass and dog faeces off his clothes. Alice doesn't recognize this gesture, not this one. It occurs to Alice that he has brought it back from the world out there, their Žižkov garden is no longer good enough, clean enough for him — and that grieves her more than their futile lovemaking.

Alice Davidovič returns along the Olšany pond alone, she passes St Roch's chapel, she walks uphill along the Olšany Cemetery dragging her feet at every step. She cradles the Sabbath tablecloth as if the youngest Davidovič were still asleep there. Every now and then she gently rocks the tablecloth, singing softly.

I am Benjamin Davidovič, the last of the Davidovič line, a little

Persian lamb never even born, a little lamb never even conceived. I am a life sacrificed twice over. I await my resurrection, for mine is the kingdom of Olšany.

THE TALE OF BENJAMIN'S KINGDOM

On the day that brought an end to Alice Davidovič's waiting, when she finally met Pavel Santner on top of Gallows Hill, and on the day that Benjamin, the last of the Davidovič line, disappeared, it is quiet in the lightwell for the first time in many years. Grandmother Davidovič opens wide the little window and lets the air from the lightwell stream into the pantry. The old folks have been needing it badly, for it so happens that without the lightwell air, which sometimes mingles with a bit of smoke from the furnace room, they are like fish out of water. Now inhaling deeply they're slowly coming around. Grandfather Davidovič even voices a wish to look out, just a little way, and tries to stand up on his wobbly legs. But Grandmother Davidovič sees Grandfather's wish as a mere pretext. Most likely he wants to see if Mrs Soška isn't somewhere about, not a chance, Grandmother won't let Grandfather near the window. This vexes Grandfather Davidovič and as punishment he doesn't speak to Grandmother for two days.

And so they are both quietly waiting for Alice to return from Pavel Santner, she went to show him the baby, naturally, but they're waiting in vain. Grandmother Davidovič suspects what the outcome of Alice's efforts is, she knows Alice is now out wandering somewhere and doesn't feel like coming home. And she also knows Alice no longer has a baby. Had it not been for the war, it could have all turned out differently. And finally what kind of love can there be when two lovers embrace after so many years and, on top of it all... Yet had there been no war and had Pavel Santner come to ask for Alice's hand, and had there then been a wedding, and after that had Ben, and possibly other children, been born, it might have come down to the same thing. Alice would be just as worn out as from those endless trips to Žižkov, and Pavel Santner would be returning to her lap just as drained by the world, they'd both have grown old just the same, and Alice would have grown ugly. And maybe Alice would have seen the day that Pavel Santner found some Mrs Soška just like Grandfather Davidovič, he'd be sure to find one.

Every now and then Grandmother Davidovič wipes away a tear, furtively, so that Grandfather Davidovič won't upbraid her. All along he's been saying she gave Alice too much freedom, and this is the result of her upbringing. Grandmother Davidovič knows Hergesell took away their Benjamin while Alice was in Pavel Santner's arms on top of Gallows Hill. She sensed it happening from the very beginning, it had to happen, and there was no use trying to prevent Alice from making that trip. She would have gone no matter what, no one could have talked her out of it, she'd been waiting all those years. And now the poor thing is wandering somewhere, searching. Yet she's no longer searching for Pavel Santner, but for Benjamin, whom she forgot because of her lover. She's ready to go all the way to Germany, all the way to Jena, where Hergesell has flown because his family lives there.

Grandfather Davidovič pretends none of this concerns him, that it's purely the result of Grandmother's bad upbringing. Except in those days he was with Mrs Soška, digging in her little garden on the outskirts of Prague instead of bringing up Alice, Grandmother doesn't fail to remind him even this time. Be that as it may, Grandfather nevertheless keeps thinking of Alice all the time. — If only he had taken Diviš instead. Why did it have to be Benjamin? People say Diviš is his anyway, and not the Lutheran's. But whenever a sacrifice is called for, the victim is always a Jew, even though he may have nothing to do with it, that's how it is.

Grandfather Davidovič is absolutely right, and all Grandmother's talk about the chosen one and the sacrificed one, about the tale of the kingdom that will arrive with his second coming, won't change a thing. Once in a while Grandmother Davidovič lets herself be carried away by her imagination to such a degree that she begins to describe how it will be when they no longer have to live in the pantry (although she's actually rather afraid, since out there lurks Mrs Soška, waiting to snatch Grandfather away). They'll go out again and take a walk, maybe to Hagibor, no, not to Hagibor, it holds such horrible memories for Grandfather. Certainly then everything will be as before, when they were still young and Grandfather was in love with Grandmother and wasn't going to Mrs Soška's, because in Benjamin's kingdom there won't even be a Mrs Soška.

THE PROCESS OF RENEWAL

Springtime brings about the process of renewal. Like the phoenix, the nation burns on a pyre and rises from its ashes. It is building a nest at the Castle, in the Spanish Hall, but it is also building one in Chapaev (formerly Lobkowicz) Square, in Kouřim Street, and even in Zásmuky Lane, which runs perpendicular to the cemetery wall. The nation is fluffing its red-blue-and-white feathers at the Castle, and it fluffs them at Olšany too.

The renewed Caretaker Briar gloats in Thomas Hamza's tobacco shop. Hamza, however, eyes him with suspicion. What if the process of renewal turns out to be like the story of the muff made of the little unborn lamb's skin? It was a stolen muff after all, it was. When even Mr Köck, however, comes in talking about it (by the way, he's no longer angry at Thomas Hamza for having sold him the muff during the war, nor for how badly the whole business ended), Thomas Hamza slowly begins to cast off his doubts.

There are numerous other signs indicating that the good old times are coming back. The young Bubeník is reopening his father's pub. Oh, that's something for Georgie Briar, Diviš takes him there just like Alice used to do, Georgie is fluffing up his briary feathers and observes his renewed image in the shiny surface of the counter. The dark period of winter sleep on the sofa is over, Georgie is full of spring fever and strange expectations.

Cerberus Briar keeps running to the little window that opens onto the hallway, keeping an eye on who enters the house. What if Herr Hergesell should rise from the dead? And he keeps thoroughly airing the flat, for it seems to him that besides the smell of yesterday's cabbage, there is still the smell of Russian tobacco, of iodine, and of the American chocolate the two liberators left lying on the table that day. And then that damned muff must be here somewhere, all these years Caretaker Briar hasn't been able to find out where Georgie hid it, Georgie won't tell, Georgie pretends he doesn't understand a thing. Caretaker Briar senses the muff is somewhere nearby, quite nearby. And during that time the memorable inscription and the view of Mount Salavat-dag disappear from his record book.

The greatest changes, however, are happening in the pantry. For the first time in more than twenty years, Grandfather Davidovič stands up and runs away from Grandmother Davidovič to Mrs Soška's. But Grandmother Davidovič knows: in the end he'll come back again, in the end they'll knock off his coxcomb. Not that Grandmother would wish it on him, not even when he was caught in the street after dark and taken to Hagibor had she wished it on him — Grandmother Davidovič, long ago, simply accepted the fact that that's the way it had to be, that one spring day Grandfather Davidovič would get a second wind and take off, but in the autumn he'd be back. How could anyone expect Mrs Soška to be interested in him when he's.... And sooner or later she's bound to find out. It's this kind of renewal — springtime grass lasts as long as it lasts.

And at Hagibor, Doe feverishly hunts for old tennis balls, digging them up from the earth, and now once again he has a whole heap of them in the bushes, though they took them away from him in the fifties, a whole heap of First Republic tennis balls awaiting their great moment. Once more all in white, Doe struts around the tennis courts, gloating and fluffing his white feathers. He looks over the fence to see if by chance Doctor Pelt or Nora Pelt are playing again. And sometimes he even manages nimbly to pick up one of the balls that has flown over the fence and throws it back.

That evening in the tomb, Mr Klečka tells Mr Turk the latest news from behind the wall: Doe is picking up tennis balls again, Grandfather Davidovič has gone off to Mrs Soška's again, Bubeník has reopened the pub again, and Caretaker Briar — no, Mr Turk doesn't want to hear a thing about him, not about that one. Mr Klečka is looking forward to their rising from the dead, now that the process of renewal is here and has become so universal. But Mr Turk cuts him short: some renewal, what with all those Briars and their ilk everywhere. Nothing lasts forever, the grape pickers will be back again — the plague knaves. But Mr Klečka takes it to be just another of Mr Turk's usual grim predictions and believes they will, nevertheless, be renewed, they will arise from their ashes, their cremated ashes, and return to their nest. And he observes the melancholy angel standing by the tomb's entrance, he too is awakening from his pestilential intoxication, fluffing his feathers. He must be dreaming of his lost wing. A faint smile plays on the melancholy angel's lips. Doesn't Mr Turk see all this? And Mr Klečka feels they don't understand each other as well as they once did, and for the first time he considers how he might leave Mr Turk. There's no way Mr Turk can convince Mr Klečka it isn't spring all around them, no way now. If only the Persian lamb muff, still damp, weren't lying hidden somewhere nearby, if only there weren't all these Briars lurking about, ready to stab with their pin.

JENA

As Herr Hergesell flies through the air with little Benjamin, he feels like an eagle or a hawk in a medieval romance, who always snatches a pouch with a ring or some other precious object from unsuspecting lovers. And the lovers whom fate has separated then wander the world over, where everything seems to be at their fingertips, in pursuit of the eagle or the hawk, but in vain. And in the end the eagle or the hawk drops the object when it discovers it's not a piece of meat. And the object falls into the ocean where a fish happens to swallow it, and some years later a fisherman happens to catch the fish, and as he prepares it, the ring falls out of the fish, and the lovers just happen to be right there, finally they recognize each other and there is a wedding. They are both still young and beautiful, despite the many years gone by, and despite all the many troubles they have endured in the world.

As the imperial eagle circles above the Vltava River, a thought occurs to him: what if he too were to drop his burden into the water. But he realizes at once that a fish would promptly swim by and swallow Benjamin, and then someone would catch the fish, and it would finally end up on the pantry table in the flat across from the Olšany Cemetery. And Hergesell realizes that whether he drops Benjamin, the unborn one, into the Vltava or not, Benjamin will return to where he has come from just the same, perhaps only as a dream flickering brightly in someone's mind and then fading away. And the eagle describes a circle in the air and descends with Benjamin to the wasteland called Hagibor. And there he leaves the child at the mercy of wild nature, at the mercy of the Olšany souls who have a chance to decide his fate for themselves. The imperial eagle ascends again, heading for Jena, his native city.

And just as the eagle is flying through St John's Gate in Jena, he collides with the 19th-century poet, Jan Kollár, who is heading for Wartburg, where a festive procession is underway. Maybe he hopes to meet Mina there, or else Friederike Schmidt. That's the way it is — the poet is flying to Lobeda to meet Mina, meanwhile she has long been lying beside him at Olšany. If only Mina had not grown so old, if only the poet had not met Hergesell the eagle at that gate, if only the Slavs at the Olšany Cemetery were not so confined, so unbearably confined.

Meanwhile in the house where Martin Luther spent a night in 1522, Hergesell's widow opens a window because she is having trouble breathing. And suddenly the room is filled with some bygone smell. She always said they had no business moving into a flat after some Jewish tenants, now that onion smell has made it all the way here. Hergesell's widow doesn't realize she smells it because Herr Hergesell is not far away, and death too is already near.

THE NATIONAL REVIVAL

The process of renewal at the Olšany Cemetery continues, Mr Turk's grim predictions will not stop it. As Mr Klečka wanders among the graves during the day, he keeps finding more and more unmistakable signs of its progress. He notices that the 19th-century linguist, Mr Šafařík, has begun a frantic search for his contemporary, Mr Palacký (what has become of that historian, the one they call the 'father of the nation'?), and keeps repeating something about the rule of bayonets and spies that has gone to its grave. Mr Kollár pines for his Mina, though she has been sleeping her eternal sleep by his side for ages, and the linguist Mr Jungmann holds forth on the Czech language from atop the graves. And graveyard poetry flourishes all around. From this Mr Klečka concludes that a time of national revival is at hand once more. One day he runs into Mr Havlíček, the sharp-tongued journalist, smiling ironically. And lots of squirrels frolic all around, even scampering at Mr Klečka's feet because they remember how he used to throw them breadcrumbs. The entire cemetery is undergoing a revival and Mr Klečka walks around as if in a daze. He no longer mentions anything to Mr Turk lest he spoil his pleasure once again. Mr Turk would probably get along well with that Havlíček fellow, those two would hit it off.

On his round, Mr Klečka gets as far as the lower part of the cemetery where he runs into Mr Sabina. Mr Sabina, one of the last century's writers, somehow seems to be hiding, as though he were not quite sure whether this process of renewal also applies to traitors and informers, and if so, in what way. And Mr Klečka almost feels sorry for Mr Sabina. — What's done is done, Mr Sabina, he tells him. — Who could hold it against you when you had a large family to feed. But Mr Sabina just sadly shakes his head. — I'm surprised you should be saying this to me, Mr Klečka, you who have had such an unhappy experience with informers, that you of all people should want to forgive me. All of those — and Mr Sabina gestures with a hand clutching his mouse-grey hat — they will never forgive me. Mr Klečka would like to persuade Mr Sabina otherwise, he would like to explain to him that now everything is different, that human sins and good deeds will now be weighed on different scales, with greater justice, but he sees Mr Sabina already moving away from him, head bowed low, and he keeps glancing about furtively to see if anyone is watching.

The encounter with Mr Sabina has nonetheless put Mr Klečka into a somewhat dejected mood, which he is unable to overcome even that evening in the presence of Mr Turk. And he ends up telling Mr Turk everything — about the national revival, about Mr Šafařík, about Mr Kollár, about Mr Jungmann, all of whom they had studied in school, although later on they were involved exclusively in the study of insects, especially silkworms, at the Institute of Entomology. Mr Klečka also mentions Mr Havlíček and his ironic smile. And Mr Turk nods his head. — That one knows, that Havlíček fellow. And Mr Klečka sees he was right, those two national prophets of doom would really hit it off. For the longest time Mr Klečka ponders whether to mention Mr Sabina, lest Mr Turk should go at it again — Some revival, what with all those Briars and their ilk everywhere, even here in the cemetery. But in the end Mr Turk gets it all out of Mr Klečka anyway. And then, surprisingly, Mr Turk says something altogether different: There you have it, that national revival of yours. First they almost let him starve to death, and then the minute he sold them the skin off his back, they condemned him unanimously.

While Mr Turk and Mr Klečka are having their talk in the tomb without paying much attention to potential eavesdroppers, Mr Sabina, traitor to his nation, slinks along among the graves, even now after dark he doesn't feel much safer, at any moment he could bump into somebody who would throw his treason in his face, almost everyone here in the cemetery knows about it, the entire Olšany Cemetery is against him, the entire nation that is so miraculously reviving itself just now.

NANYNKA SHMID'S SLEEP

Once again it is early summer at Olšany, once again a ship lies at anchor in the square, her white masts swaying in the wind, and at the top the Shmids are doing handstands — not the brothers Shmid any more, Karel of course fell to his death, but Shmid father and son. Adults pay three crowns each, children one crown, and for those like Thomas Hamza, who happen to have windows overlooking the square, the show is free of charge. Diviš is here and Alice too, they can't take their eyes off the two men up there. And Nanynka Shmid has also come to watch. Diviš knows Nanynka is dead, he and his whole class attended her funeral, she was run over by a car. He had called to her and she ran to him across the street. And the milk spilled all over the road, and Nanynka's life seeped away in the milky trickle. It was then that Diviš finally understood why Nanynka was afraid down on the ground but not up there, down here it really was altogether different.

Nanynka Shmid has since grown up, she's completely transformed, but the scent of country fairs has stayed with her, it is mixed with the smell of milk and a faint aroma of the Olšany wine. Diviš is attracted by Nanynka's scent, now even more than years ago. And Diviš leans toward Nanynka and says: Nanynka, you smell so good. But his words make Nanynka start, as if she didn't like being addressed by Diviš, as if she didn't even recognize him. So Diviš reminds her: Don't you remember me, Nanynka, we used to go fetch milk together, and you always carried a blue pitcher. But then Diviš stops short, realizing he shouldn't have said this, of all things not this.

And Nanynka Shmid really is sorry that Diviš reminded her of this, this of all things, and she's on the verge of tears. And Diviš gently caresses Nanynka's hair and apologizes, he didn't mean it that way. Just at that moment the Shmids are sliding down the white masts to the ground, and Nanynka breathes a sigh of relief, happy that her father and her brother are done for the day. Maybe that's why she also forgives Diviš and even smiles at him through her tears. — Do you remember, Nanynka, how we played cops and robbers and hid in a tomb? Diviš couldn't have said anything worse, yet he was actually hoping this memory would bring them closer. Can't Diviš understand how Nanynka feels when now she has to be there all the time? Doesn't he remember how afraid she was even then, when she and Diviš used to hide there, doesn't he recall how anxious she was? And now of course it's worse, much worse.

Nanynka runs away from Diviš in tears, but he follows her everywhere, he'd like to apologize again but where could he find words kind enough for her, now that Nanynka no longer trusts him. She runs down Kouřim Street and up Zásmuky Lane, but there Diviš catches up with her and won't let her go. And Nanynka, held in his embrace, suddenly becomes meek as a lamb, she even cuddles up to Diviš, nestles in his arms and hides her head under his reindeer sweater, so as not to see the cemetery across from them. And Diviš gently reprimands her, she can't carry on like this, she must return there, and if she wishes, he'll accompany her. And Nanynka realizes that Diviš is just like everyone else, both living and dead. Yet she lets Diviš lead her, for she is too weak to oppose him. But why hadn't Diviš been holding her then, why was he on the other side of the street, why did he call to her from there, why did he let her life seep away in that milky trickle?

Once more, Diviš and Nanynka jump off the cemetery wall with their eyes closed, and backwards. This time, however, their fingers don't sink into the soil, for a long time now there has been a drought, the earth is parched and hard as stone. Diviš lightly scrapes the skin of his fingertips, and tiny particles of the Olšany soil enter his blood. Nanynka doesn't fail to notice this, but Diviš doesn't know yet, not yet. Diviš wants them to go and look at the place where they had been together before, but Nanynka is afraid. Yet what can Nanynka still be afraid of? Nanynka knows that Mr Turk is in the tomb, and she is afraid of Mr Turk because he is said to be odd. Yet what can Nanynka do when Diviš is pulling her by the hand and resisting him is so hard.

Mr Turk is standing by the tomb's entrance, motioning them to come in. — Isn't this Nanynka Shmid, and that's Diviš Paskal, they'd all met here once before, but that time Diviš hadn't noticed Mr Turk. — It wasn't your fault, Mr Diviš, no need to apologize.

And while Mr Turk and Diviš are talking, Nanynka falls asleep on Diviš's lap because she is very tired. And then Mr Turk asks Diviš why he came all this way with Nanynka, and what his intentions with her are. — You know, Mr Diviš, Nanynka isn't the same as she was then, don't you see how tired she is from the trip, and you're also partly to blame, you too. Once you're gone and she wakes up, she'll feel even sadder than before, being here will become even more difficult for her. Have you considered, Mr Diviš, what it's like for her, to be caught between two worlds, between two abysses, when first you take her in your arms and then let her fall again? Don't ever come back, Mr Diviš, if you ever loved Nanynka and if you mean well for her, don't ever torture her again. Do go now, Mr Diviš, farewell.

Diviš carefully puts Nanynka down on the ground, and she doesn't even wake up, she goes on sleeping, she must be very tired, and Diviš promises Mr Turk never to come back, he can trust his word, it had never occurred to him, it won't happen again. As Diviš moves away, he notices Nanynka's scent slowly disappearing, soon he is no longer sure whether he smells Nanynka's fragrance or the scent of Olšany. And as Diviš crosses the road, he sees a milky trickle running over it once more, and seeping away in that trickle… this time it's not Nanynka's life, but Nanynka's death, the sleep of death that overcame her there beyond the wall. And since the scent doesn't reach this far, Diviš is no longer thinking of Nanynka, he has stopped loving her again.

THE TRAITOR OF THE NATION'S HAT

The news is spreading from grave to grave: There is a traitor of
the nation in the cemetery. Nobody knows who was the first to
hear. Wasn't it Mr Klečka? But he has only confided in Mr Turk,
and whom would Mr Turk tell? Evidently Mr Klečka was neither
the first nor the last to see Mr Sabina, even graves have eyes and
ears. Certainly Mr Erben has instructed his daughter not to say
anything of importance in front of Eufrosina, Mr Sabina's daughter.
By that Mr Erben meant no harm to Mr Sabina, and neither did
Mr Klečka, but be this as it may, it was they, after all, who drew
attention to him.

And now the chase is on at the Olšany Cemetery. Sabina is seen
here, and then again there, he zigzags among the graves and hides
behind the gravestones. From time to time Mr Sabina commits the
error of hiding behind the tombstone of a national revivalist, and
then has a hard time getting him off his back. His safest choice is
to hide behind children's graves (if only their gravestones weren't
so low). And if graves of unborn children existed, for example a
little grave of Benjamin Davidovič abandoned in the wasteland
of Hagibor, Mr Sabina would have hidden behind it. But who
knows where the last of the Davidovič line has gone, the little
Jewish lamb never even conceived?

And as Mr Sabina cowers behind one of the children's graves
and brushes against it, Nanynka Shmid speaks to him. She feels
sorry for Mr Sabina, who is trembling all over and keeps looking
around with trepidation. Nanynka Shmid recognizes Mr Sabina,
although his picture was not in the textbooks of her generation, the
dead sense everything, recognize everything, and know everything
that relates to them, and Mr Sabina's hand did touch her gravestone. Nanynka Shmid can relate to Mr Sabina's fear, she too is
afraid in the cemetery, because down here everything is different

from up there. And she remembers her benefactor, Mr Turk, and how she fell asleep in his tomb after her meeting with Diviš Paskal, when a terrible fatigue overcame her. She didn't even know what it was that had made her so tired, it was only a few steps from the cemetery to the square, and then she just went down Kouřim Street and up Zásmuky Lane, back to the cemetery. She vaguely remembers Diviš saying something hurtful to her along the way, which made her so sad she couldn't hold back her tears. But then cuddling up to Diviš as he held her in his arms, and hiding her head under his reindeer sweater so as not to see the cemetery, all that felt so strangely pleasant. And Nanynka woke up only that night, Mr Klečka was bending over her speaking in a kind voice. And Mr Turk explained to Nanynka that he had sent Diviš away because it was better that way for both of them (even Nanynka knew it was better that way), and he tried to talk her into being sensible from now on and not going to the square even when her father and brother were climbing up the masts and doing handstands at the top, she could see them quite well from here too. And Nanynka promised to be sensible and never again to go to the square, but to watch only from here.

Nanynka slowly recalls all this as she notices Mr Sabina trembling with fear behind her gravestone. She tells him she knows some good people, they're staying in that tomb over there, and there's sure to be room for him too, Nanynka will take him there. And as soon as Nanynka pronounces the names of Mr Turk and Mr Klečka, Mr Sabina cheers up a little and says: I know Mr Klečka. Mr Sabina thanks Nanynka nicely, saying he'll go there at once, he knows the way, she needn't go with him. And only when Mr Sabina is far away does Nanynka notice his hat lying on the ground, a shabby, mouse-grey hat, by now almost shapeless. And as Nanynka touches the hat, it seems to her to be quite frightened too, and so she puts it in her lap. She is holding in her lap the hat that belongs to Mr Sabina, the hat that belongs to the traitor of the nation. And that Nanynka Shmid should not have done.

Meanwhile Mr Sabina reaches the tomb of Mr Turk and Mr

Klečka. They see him coming from afar, they are expecting him. Mr Turk figured right away that one day Mr Sabina would come to seek refuge with them, since Mr Klečka didn't condemn him that day. Mr Sabina bows with humility. He was sent by the acrobats' little girl. Mr Klečka wants to ask Mr Sabina to come in, but Mr Turk steps in front of him and says to Mr Sabina: My dear Mr Sabina, what you have done is all the same to me, I won't go into what I think about it at this time. But I won't let you in. Not because you are Sabina, I'd say the same thing to anyone else in your place. It would be of no use, I used to hide in here myself and you probably know what happened to me. And to Mr Klečka too, though he is much younger. He would now happily invite you in, for he still knows too little about life and death, and still has all sorts of illusions. Find yourself someone else and leave us alone, we've been through enough.

At Mr Turk's words Mr Sabina completely curls up into himself and is about to leave, when he discovers his hat missing and begs to be allowed to look around for it, it was a mouse-grey hat, actually quite ancient, but he has no other. And as the three of them look for the hat, they suddenly notice graves all around them coming to life and moving towards them. And at that moment it occurs to Mr Turk that Mr Sabina may have invented the story of the hat (Mr Turk is almost certain he hadn't seen any hat), because he already knew they were at his heels. But now it's too late, their quiet life is over, even if Mr Sabina left now, everyone would know that he'd been hiding with them. And for the second time Mr Turk feels sorry for Mr Klečka, who really is so much younger, and who in his company seems to have had nothing but bad luck, and now he's about to lose some more of his illusions.

Who could hold it against Mr Turk that after all he has experienced, he's become craven and hardly seems disturbed by the sight of the dead going after Mr Sabina, tossing him about like a tennis ball, and finally throwing the traitor of the nation over the wall, leaving him to his fate. The cemetery is pure again, the black sheep has been cast out, the process of renewal may continue. But then somebody notices the mouse-grey hat, Nanynka Shmid, the acrobats' little girl, is holding it in her lap. Yet as they try to take it from her, Nanynka won't let go of it, she grasps the hat tightly. She should think it over, they saw her walking hand in hand with that Diviš, who's trying to beguile his way into their ranks, that bastard, that posthumous wolf cub. They saw only too clearly her attempts to deny the cemetery, hiding her head under that bastard's sweater. And Nanynka, not quite knowing what possesses her, throws the hat upward with all her might, and the hat flies, flies all the way to the top of the mast where her father does handstands every night, and there the hat stays dangling.

The traitor of the nation's hat dangles high above Chapaev Square, high above Olšany, there it swivels in the wind like a weathervane. The hat blows with the wind, for it is an informer's hat, the hat of a turncoat.

Mr Sabina climbs up to the fifth floor with difficulty. He walks quickly past the pantry, you can't trust anybody these days, not even Grandmother and Grandfather Davidovič. Mr Sabina doesn't really know why he set out to find refuge precisely here, perhaps he heard of Diviš's cemetery experience, perhaps he was hoping to find a kindred soul here. And maybe, rather than coming to see Diviš, he's here to see Diviš's father, Jan Paskal.

— Roman, I've been expecting you for a long time, Jan Paskal says and motions Mr Sabina to sit down. Mr Sabina isn't even surprised that Paskal knows his code name, he must have heard it from Messrs Horngoat and Hoardgold, they mentioned Sabina's case in his presence. Mr Sabina and Jan Paskal then sit opposite each other, saying nothing, only observing one another. Mr Sabina notices that every now and then Jan Paskal touches his neck, as if a tight collar were choking him. And Jan Paskal looks at Mr Sabina's worn shoes and shabby coat, stained in several spots with Olšany wine. And he doesn't fail to notice that Mr Sabina has lost his hat.

— Roman, you can spend the night, you can't go back there. Look, it's beginning to rain ... But Mr Sabina shakes his head: Oh no, but thank you very much for your hospitality. I'll just warm up a little and then go. And Mr Sabina gets ready to leave, searching all around for his hat. — It was a mouse-grey hat. Jan Paskal helps him look for it, although he knows Mr Sabina had arrived without a hat. And as they are both busy searching, Horngoat and Hoardgold suddenly appear in the doorway. Their fingers beckon to — no, not to Jan Paskal this time, today it's Mr Sabina's turn, and Jan Paskal heaves a sigh of relief. Mr Sabina still ventures to say: You must be mistaken, gentlemen, I am actually no longer…, but they aren't paying attention and just grab hold of his arms, one on each side. — Come on now, Roman, don't fuss. Without any warning, Mr Sabina finds himself in the grip of the two voids from Bartholomew Street. And at that moment Mr Sabina notices a bulge under the front of Horngoat's coat, as if he were hiding something there. That must be it, they've got his hat, he left it somewhere, and because of the hat they found him, because of the hat. But where on earth did he leave it?

And a moment later, as Nanynka Shmid looks up, she sees that the hat is gone from the mast. And it makes her happy because she assumes the hat has returned to its owner. And she is right, indeed it has. Yet at what cost?

RETURN OF THE PLAGUE KNAVES

One summer night Mr Klečka goes out as usual to get some fresh graveyard air. And once more he runs into Mr Havlíček. This time Mr Havlíček isn't smiling, and moreover he unexpectedly addresses Mr Klečka: My friend, disaster is near, for Schmerling's been here. Mr Klečka doesn't understand a thing, he can only guess that Mr Havlíček is again prophesying doom, like Mr Turk, and in rhymed verse at that.

— Mr Havlíček, have you heard that Mr Sabina… Mr Klečka can't hold back, he can't help it, that's his nature, and he tells Mr Havlíček the whole story. Mr Havlíček just smiles bitterly and once more prophesies doom: Not just a disaster, but worse! Mr Havlíček in fact has a premonition of Windischgrätz presently marching upon Prague, barricades will be going up again all over the city... And Mr Havlíček even seems to hear the earth rumbling under Windischgrätz's advancing artillery. And he bids Mr Klečka to put his ear to the ground to listen if the army is on its way. Mr Klečka puts his ear to the Olšany ground and listens. And he really can hear the earth rumbling, as though an abyss were about to open wide. Gehenna, Jan Paskal would say. And Mr Klečka is seized by fear, what if the entire Olšany Cemetery were to plunge into that abyss, and he hurries back to Mr Turk so they could at least be together when it happened. And strangely, no matter how sad Mr Klečka has felt at the cemetery, now that he is about to lose this garden, now that he is about to cease to exist himself — that is to exist less than now — he finds it a rather pleasant place.

And since Mr Klečka is running so fast as to get out of breath, he grows intoxicated with the Olšany fragrance, even headier now in the month of August, he totters among the graves, searching for Mr Turk. Luckily he is spotted by Nanynka Shmid, she has awakened, aroused by the distant rumbling. Nanynka takes Mr Klečka by the hand and leads him home to Mr Turk. And a multitude of startled squirrels scamper after them.

Mr Turk paces nervously up and down in front of the tomb, he is worried about Mr Klečka. The grapes have ripened once again, Mr Turk hasn't tasted them this time either, once again the grapes have grown overripe, there is a touch of putrefaction in the air, and from far away one can hear the grape pickers coming, they are riding on the carts they had used earlier for transporting corpses. And finally Mr Turk sees Mr Klečka being led by Nanynka Shmid. For heaven's sake, what has happened to Mr Klečka, why is he tottering like a drunkard? And the squirrels, as though having gone mad, grow ever more brazen, flinging themselves into the air, leaping up into Mr Klečka's face, and shrieking. But where is Mr Klečka to get bread now? And Nanynka Shmid shoos the brazen squirrels away because Mr Klečka doesn't have the heart to do so, and besides he's in a daze.

Finally the two are together again. Mr Klečka is babbling something about a certain Schmerling, and Mr Turk doesn't understand what this has to do with the rumbling earth. And it occurs to him that perhaps Mr Klečka has tasted the Olšany wine, he who had never even touched wine. Indeed this night will not be short, muses Mr Turk as he puts Mr Klečka to bed in the tomb, covering him with the old loden coat.

Dawn is breaking at Olšany as the plague knaves reach the city. By now their carts are encamped at the Castle and thunder down Stalin Avenue (now actually Vinohradská), Kostya Sukhoruchkov is riding in one of them and Georgie Briar is running towards him. Kostya Sukhoruchkov recognizes Georgie because Georgie has been cursed into the form of an eternal child, and Georgie recognizes Kostya Sukhoruchkov, it seems like yesterday that Kostya Sukhoruchkov was sitting beside him on the sofa, feeding him American chocolate. But Kostya Sukhoruchkov doesn't stop, he continues in the direction of Hagibor, pretending not to know Georgie, and Georgie Briar rolls a pin in the palm of his hand.

And just then Grandfather Davidovič happens to be walking by, he's returning from Mrs Soška's, and it occurs to him they might want to arrest him as before and take him again to Hagibor and break him on the wheel. But they pay no attention to him and keep rumbling on. And Grandmother Davidovič throws up her hands in disbelief: So you're back again, you won't make trouble for a while. And Grandfather Davidovič, all meek and silent, is glad to be back in the pantry with Grandmother Davidovič, what with the plague knaves on the loose outside, and happy that Grandmother won't turn him out.

In the general chaos that set in after the arrival of the plague knaves at Olšany (and also in the Spanish Hall of the Castle), it is difficult to distinguish the boundary between the world of the living and the dead, separated till now by the cemetery wall. The two worlds have begun to merge more than ever before. Some souls have run out of the cemetery and mingled with the crowd where Caretaker Briar, Mr Köck and, a little farther back, Thomas Hamza are lingering. All the way up front stands Doe, the ball boy from the time of the First Republic, his coat strangely bulging at the sides. Every so often he reaches into his pockets and throws a tennis ball at a passing plague cart. And the tennis ball from the golden age always bounces off the cart and onto the heads of the spectators. One tennis ball falls at Thomas Hamza's feet. Thomas Hamza touches it very lightly with the tip of his shoe, one never knows what to expect from such a tennis ball, and then kicks it away as far as he can. The tennis ball flies low over the ground in the direction of the cemetery and hits one of Mrs Havlíček's knees. Mrs Havlíček utters a cry and falls down, but quickly gets up again and hurries over to Thomas Hamza who is standing way in the back.

— Excuse me, but have you seen my Karel? And as she questions Thomas Hamza, there comes another tennis ball that has just bounced off the cart carrying Kostya Sukhoruchkov and hits Mrs Havlíček in the mouth. Thomas Hamza stares in disbelief at the trickle of blood running slowly down her chin. Alas, Thomas Hamza hasn't seen her Karel. — I'm terribly sorry, Mrs Havlíček, I hope you find your little boy soon. And he offers her his silk handkerchief to wipe off the blood, people are being uncommonly considerate toward one another today, even Thomas Hamza is being considerate. Mrs Havlíček takes the handkerchief but neither says thank you nor wipes away the trickle of blood. Instead she begins to wave the handkerchief above her head so that people make way for her, and she gets through to the the front of the crowd where Caretaker Briar, Mr Köck and also Doe, the one who keeps throwing the tennis balls, are standing. — Gentlemen, haven't you seen Karel Havlíček? Caretaker Briar knows one Havlíček, a former school janitor, but his first name isn't Karel. And Mr Köck tries to snatch the white handkerchief from her hand because it looks as if she's offering to surrender. Meanwhile Mrs Havlíček is thinking: Haven't I already surrendered? If only it had done any good. And she clutches the handkerchief firmly. At that moment Doe turns to her and says: Karel Havlíček? Why, they've taken him to Brixen! Mrs Havlíček is devastated by Doe's news, although she suspected as much. And if it hadn't been for Alice Davidovič, who suddenly appeared next to her and drew her aside, Mrs Havlíček would have collapsed in the middle of the street.

When Thomas Hamza offered Mrs Havlíček his silk handkerchief, he felt a surge of infinite goodness and moral nobility inside. It was the trickle of blood on Mrs Havlíček's chin that touched him so. And he also felt sorry for her because she had lost her little boy, perhaps she would find him in the end. But before long Thomas Hamza is overcome with regret, it was a nice handkerchief, a silk one (how many silkworm cocoons had gone into making it, perhaps Mr Klečka or Mr Turk could calculate that), and she may very well just toss it somewhere along the way, she was acting rather confused. What a pity, such a fine handkerchief.

But Thomas Hamza is very wrong to think Mrs Havlíček will just toss his handkerchief somewhere along the way. Mrs Havlíček can guess the value of such a handkerchief, not because it's made of silk (how many unborn moths did it take to make it), but because this piece of silk is from the other side — from over there. When Mr Köck tried to snatch it from her, fearing she might surrender to the plague knaves, for that's what Mr Turk would call all foreign invaders, she firmly clutched that piece of silk from the other world. Maybe she believed it would help her obtain a pardon for Karel Havlíček, who had been taken to Brixen again. Maybe she thought she could use the handkerchief for ransom.

And as the profoundly depressed Mrs Havlíček sits on the

ground by the cemetery wall with Alice Davidovič and puts the silk to her face, she is overcome by a deep nostalgia, a yearning for the world and for life. Alice Davidovič senses this, she understands how Mrs Havlíček feels, Alice knows this yearning, this nostalgia, very well. She tells her gently: It's the handkerchief, Mrs Havlíček. Throw it away and the feeling will pass. But Mrs Havlíček shakes her head. Nobody really knows what power it may possess. She will take the handkerchief to Brixen, what if Dedera, the police commissioner, can be appeased (it was certainly he who had taken Havlíček away again). Alice Davidovič has her own ideas about this. How could Mrs Havlíček make it all the way to Brixen, when even a short walk has left her completely exhausted? Why would Dedera be appeased by Thomas Hamza's handkerchief? But Alice Davidovič doesn't want to crush Mrs Havlíček's hopes and so she says to her: Mrs Havlíček, of course you'll go to Brixen, but only in the morning, now you must rest. And she helps Mrs Havlíček to her feet.

And Mrs Havlíček is quite glad she doesn't have to go now, she won't go until morning, because she can hardly stand up. They have gone only a few steps when Nanynka Shmid notices them. The moment Nanynka spots the silk handkerchief, she grows lively because she likes pretty things. When Mrs Havlíček sees how much Nanynka Shmid desires this silken piece of the world, she gives her the handkerchief, after all she had met with such a sad fate while fetching milk and still a mere a child. As Mrs Havlíček presses the handkerchief into Nanynka's hand, she feels rather sorry. Now that she doesn't have the little scrap, Dedera can hardly be appeased. No sooner does she relinquish the piece of silk, all her nostalgia suddenly vanishes, life and the world appear to her again as worthless as they did before she touched them in the handkerchief. And with the ever fading memory of the intoxicating silken softness of the little roll in which the world was wrapped up like a silkworm, *Bombyx mori*, and whose softness rivalled that of Alice's Persian lamb muff, Mrs Havlíček begins to realize very clearly that she won't be going to Brixen the next morning either, it wouldn't do any good anyway. Dederas cannot be appeased by anything, let alone by Thomas Hamza's handkerchief, even if it held the whole world, impatiently awaiting its metamorphosis into a butterfly.

BOMBYX MORI

I am *Bombyx mori*, the silkworm, the mulberry bombycid, a night moth of the family Bombycidae. I am the egg from which the caterpillar hatches in early spring. The caterpillar sheds its skin four times before maturing into an adult, before forming a cocoon, before becoming a pupa. And this is how it is done: through two orifices in my lower lip I let out a fibrous filament that I keep winding around myself for several days. I am the caterpillar of *Bombyx mori*, I take three days to form my cocoon, and in five days I change into a pupa. I am a pupa and I rest inside my cocoon for two to three weeks. And I will let you in on a secret: of the three layers of my cocoon, the finest is the second one from which silk is spun. But where has my silk gone, where is the night moth into which I was supposed to change? — They placed the cocoon in a hot oven, then placed it in hot water, then spun it into silk fibre, then wove the fibre into — a handkerchief. Alas, poor cocoon, alas, poor unborn moth!

How hungry I was as a caterpillar! So many leaves, so many mulberry leaves did I consume, the anxiety I felt during the fast preceding the great moment of initiating my cocoon. It took me the longest time to find an appropriate place to do it. All that changing! And then, finally, my great day arrived, I was growing intoxicated by the two trickles of silk flowing from my mouth, I kept fastening them around my body like so many belts, and thus decked out, I changed into a pupa, into my own mummy awaiting its mysterious metamorphosis, its resurrection in a different time, a time of moths and butterflies.

I am the moth, the imago of *Bombyx mori*. Oh, how I scorn my former baldness, my previous wingless existence, my past life as a caterpillar! To have wings and fly — what a vertiginous feeling! Is it still me, *Bombyx mori*, does a moth have anything whatsoever in common with a caterpillar? There is just a faded memory, a nebulous memory of something creeping, of something sticky. Who can prove to me now that the caterpillar and the moth are my two likenesses, that my life is split into two such opposite existences, and that there is still the dark period of the cocoon when the miracle of transubstantiation takes place?

I am *Bombyx mori*. If only there hadn't been that caterpillar forming the cocoon. And if only there hadn't been that silk for which I was sacrificed, I, silk moth *Bombyx mori* not yet born.

DESCENT INTO THE MOUNTAIN

Jan Tůňka, the youngest of the Tůňka boys, always has his head filled with dreams and fantasies. And it's also filled with a yearning for which his crude brothers have no understanding, and neither does Mařenka, his sister. Jan Tůňka is lying in the hayloft of the house where he was born in Karhule, dreaming. And sometimes he converses with František. He keeps planning to go and enter the mountain, for where else but there can he find his father. The dead from Karhule, his father used to say, don't go to the cemetery but into the mountain instead. And were a living person to enter it, he would never return, except perhaps when...

Private Jan Tůňka is lying in a tent and dreaming about the mountain again. Suddenly he seems to see someone lift the corner of the canvas and peer in. It is František, his prematurely born nephew, by now he must be at least nine years old. Most likely the time has come to enter the mountain, most likely Father has sent František to fetch his youngest son, to take him away from the military camp, past the dozing guards. The camp is full of foreign soldiers, maybe even Kostya Sukhoruchkov is among them. Private Jan Tůňka doesn't know why the foreign soldiers

are here, but it's better not to ask, they might laugh at him. —
A knight of Blaník Mountain! Even the lieutenant laughed at that.
But it's not advisable to mock the mountain, as Father used to
say, one never knows what the mountain may do.

Jan Tůňka suspects that František is waiting for him in front of
the tent, so he hastily gets dressed. To make less noise as he walks,
he picks up his boots and carries them in one hand. In the other
he holds the belt he'll use to lower himself into the mountain. The
mountain has come all this way to him, he feels it pulling him
down, but his feet are still groping in space, unable to find the
bottom. The mountain must be deeper than he thought. František
has already made it all the way down and keeps encouraging him:
Just a bit more. But it's precisely this bit that lies between life and
death. If only the belt were a little longer. Tůňka is suspended
within the mountain, unable to move to or fro. He tries to hurry,
because there are swarms of soldiers all around. The lieutenant is
there too, pointing at Jan Tůňka: So this is a knight, some knight!
A hanged man!

Naturally, it never occurs to Mařenka Tůňka to bang on the
mountain and awaken the sleeping knights. The village of Karhule
is so cut off from the rest of the world that one never sees foreign
soldiers. This all touches Mařenka Tůňka's life only from far, far
away. She's more disturbed by the strange goings-on that had
begun this summer in the hayloft. One morning Mařenka goes
up as usual to get her dry laundry, and suddenly she seems to
see something stir in the hay. As if someone had sighed in his
sleep, perhaps having a bad dream. Only a few weeks back, her
youngest brother Jan was sleeping in exactly that spot, before
he was drafted, the imprint of his body is still visible in the hay.
Each time Mařenka has gone up to the hayloft, she has had to
pass that spot, and each time she has remembered how much her
brother wished not to serve in the army. What if Jan has come
back, maybe they let him go, took pity on him because he was
so homesick. Mařenka steps closer, she's not afraid, why should
she be afraid of her little brother, she pokes around in the hay,

but no one is there.

Mařenka Tůňka is taking down the dry laundry when she hears those sighs again, now she hears them from somewhere above her head, in the rafters. It occurs to Mařenka that perhaps it's her unborn child who haunts the hayloft, she named him František and made a bed for him in a shoe box. Maybe that baby feels hurt because she now has another little one in his place and comes up here to hang out his nappies. Of course this must hurt František. Mařenka Tůňka doesn't wonder how it could be that František is here with her when he was left behind in Prague in a shoe box, it seems natural to her he should be where she is, even if it's under the rafters. And Mařenka tries to soothe him: Hush hush, František, you're mine too. And it's as if this is what Paskal's little bastard has been waiting for, with these words he quietens, grows silent.

About ten days later, however, on the day of Jan's funeral, those sighs sounded again. Mařenka was heating up a big pot of sausages for the soldiers, a whole busload had arrived, and meanwhile she went to the hayloft to take down the laundry. Again she heard the sighs that at times sounded like a child crying. Already as she was going up there, she was somewhat afraid, as if she expected to see something terrible in the hayloft, maybe her hanged brother, though she knew very well that graveyard earth had been heaped upon him. This time Mařenka no longer dared to look even from the corner of her eye at the spot where the hay had been flattened by his body, by the body of that summertime recruit, not this time. What if both dead ones had conspired against her and were waiting for her here? But she has no time to console them now, downstairs she is heating up sausages, a whole washtub full of sausages — funeral sausages. So she just tells them: Be good and sleep well. And they really do fall silent, not even a peep.

In the village of Karhule, the lieutenant nibbles on a funeral sausage, gazing at Blaník Mountain as it slowly disappears in a milky haze. Who could have guessed that Tůňka would feel so hurt, that the country boy was such a sissy? But he doesn't mention the practical joke to Mařenka Tůňka. Who could have foreseen that Tůňka would mistake an abyss for a mountain, who would have thought that the knight from Blaník Mountain would hang himself? And Mařenka Tůňka, sitting down for a moment and looking at the soldiers and their officer eating sausages, remembers again those two up in the hayloft. She feels very anxious about all this but doesn't dare tell anyone, not even the officer who had spoken to her so nicely about Jan, not even him. She concludes that it probably must be so, that the dead stay with us, find themselves a hidden nook, perhaps in the rafters. And it's not really very strange that they need us, that they seek consolation from us, because they're so helpless and probably homesick.

DOCTOR PELT'S WINTER GARDEN

Doctor Pelt observes his Christmas tree. It is leaning to one side, already dry and decrepit, a touch of a finger would make it collapse — The tree has scoliosis, muses Doctor Pelt, and the older it gets, the worse its affliction becomes. Pelt knows this from his own experience, for the ten years he's no longer been working at the clinic, he's been propping up one side of his body with a little pillow. It has been ten years now since he was forced to leave the clinic, his dermatological paradise, his cutaneous cabinet of curiosities. Before the war, the clinic had first, second and third class rooms, plus several rooms of a deluxe A-1 category with rococo furniture and a special menu. Pelt's clinic catered to the rich and also the not so rich, for they all suffered from various dermatoses treatable by the miraculous Doctor Pelt, the renowned head physician Pelt.

And there was also a winter garden where patients could walk at leisure and discuss their skins among mother-in-law's tongue plants and paradise trees. Sometimes even the great Doctor Pelt would pass through the garden and stop to talk with psoriasis, exchange a few words with ichthyosis, and then hurry off again, for somewhere a skin was urgently awaiting him, perhaps a burned skin, or Miss Beaver's skin, still soft at the time, in a little room above the garden. — He'll let the chill in from down there, from that promised garden of his, grumbles Miss Beaver, waiting impatiently in the little room with rococo furniture.

Pelt is sitting, one side of his body propped up with a little pillow, contemplating the Christmas tree. Both he and the tree are tilting more and more. Pelt feels sorry for the Christmas tree, and he also feels sorry for himself. Suddenly, Mrs Pelt is standing next to him, the second Mrs Pelt, the one who was waiting in the rococo room. — You're sitting around in that garden of yours again. She carelessly brushes against the tree, not on purpose, oh no, and the tree, as if touched by a magic wand, suddenly stands there completely bare except for the colourful ornaments still hanging on it, now set in motion and jingling as they sway. Doctor Pelt also seems to have collapsed completely, to have abruptly shed all his hair. Huddled in his chair, denuded old Pelt sinks more and more to one side. Pelt knows she did it on purpose, she pushed it, though she may deny it now. Oh where, oh where is his garden?

And suddenly a cry: Pelt, I'm burning! — Now, in the wintertime? — Where? — Between the National Museum and the Food Bazaar. Pelt rushes to the clinic, he runs through the winter garden among his mother-in-law's tongue plants, they have grown incredibly tall in the years he's been away. There are no paradise trees, the paradise trees must have died. — Pelt, help! A skinless body is lying in an oil bath. The miraculous Doctor Pelt can only helplessly throw up his arms. And in the square below the Museum, where the fountain doesn't flow in the winter, they are already arranging a memorial service. If porridge is served to the mourners, every last one will show up.

Mr Turk says that every epoch fulfils ancient parables in its own way and in its own image. Take for example the parable of the three young men in the fiery furnace, even this one has an analogy in today's times, albeit a rather unusual one, considering that the men enter the furnace of their own free will, and not only that, they even carry the furnace along with them, like snails their shells. They are transformed into a furnace, and within that furnace they are consumed by fire. Only they don't emerge from the furnace alive and well, nor renewed, they don't rise from their ashes like some birds, instead, their remains travel to the clinic in Leger Street, or directly to the Institute of Pathology, and from there to the cemetery.

When the first young man enters his furnace, somewhere between the National Museum and the Food Bazaar (the fact that the mystery play was acted out precisely there is highly symbolic, because the nation worships both tabernacles with equal ardor), he leaves behind a legend that gradually becomes more and more a graveyard legend. When later on the second young man enters his furnace, it takes place in the lobby of the Time cinema. And when the third young man enters his furnace, it is in a place so obscure that hardly anyone notices, let alone worries about whether he comes out. But it's not even certain there was such a third young man and that he entered a furnace, because in the meantime another parable had already begun to be fulfilled — most likely the parable of the Egyptian captivity.

Mr Klečka thinks of the three young men from the fiery furnaces that Mr Turk had talked about as he tried to explain to him the tale's meaning in the context of the times. If everything were actually the way Mr Turk saw it (and one mustn't forget that his vantage point is from a tomb at Olšany), then there really would be no hope left. But Mr Klečka is still young and doesn't want simply to accept this. He decides to go to the grave of the first young man from the fiery furnace, he's still there, they haven't yet taken him to Všetaty, his hometown. Mr Klečka addresses him, but the latter remains silent, evidently taking Mr Klečka for a nosy fellow who has come to take a look at his burns. Doesn't even this young man believe in resurrection? But then the young man from the fiery furnace changes his mind after all, perhaps he realizes Mr Klečka isn't just another gawker, and he asks Mr Klečka for some water. Only it mustn't be from the cemetery's water pipe, the young man doesn't trust that water. But where else would Mr Klečka find water, if not at the Olšany pond.

But it's a long way to the pond, and the way back is even longer, and the water Mr Klečka scooped up in his hands runs out between his fingers. By the time Mr Klečka returns to the thirsting young man, there isn't even a trace of dampness in his palms. And the young man, as if he had suspected what would happen all along, just sighs: Not a drop. Just you try to stay in a fiery furnace all that time. Mr Klečka tries to explain, but the young man doesn't seem to notice him any more, and instead is thinking: Everybody remains in his furnace alone, nobody will even give you a drink of water. And the young man renounces the whole world.

For a long while afterwards, Mr Turk tries to console Mr Klečka, telling him it couldn't have ended otherwise, how could he have brought the young man water when he had to cross the whole cemetery, which now in summer is itself one big furnace, scorching everything. — Including any dreams and illusions, Mr Turk says with emphasis, because Mr Klečka is precisely one of those who keeps nurturing all kinds of hopes, but ends up lacking water, even the tiniest drop of living water.

Mr Turk's fatalism has of late become unbearable to Mr Klečka. And Mr Klečka thinks it's time to rebel against the fate constantly forced upon him by Mr Turk, to go his own way, albeit just along a graveyard path, or perhaps to set out even farther, all the way to Hagibor, Mr Turk's voice of Providence may not reach that far, not as far as that. And Mr Turk knows that Mr Klečka is contemplating a rebellion, an escape from the Olšany preserve, but he no longer says anything. He wraps himself in his companion's loden coat and grows silent.

THE GAZEBO IN STRAŠNICE

Nora Paskal observes Pelt in the crematorium in Prague's Strašnice quarter. Soon he will again be hers. Pelt is lying behind a glass partition. It seems to her that his hair is still wet from the Babylonian flood that silenced his speech *de morbis cutaneis*. Pelt himself now lies here like a specimen of skin, and all around sharp mother-in-law's tongues protrude upwards. They remind her of Pelt's winter garden, only the paradise trees with their tiny red apples are missing.

Once little Nora had the idea of hiding behind those sharp tongues. She waited there for Pelt to pass through the winter garden on his way to the upper rooms. From afar she could recognize Pelt's voice, the torrent of words, dermatological words, surging through the corridor, suffocating Pelt's retinue of disciples. As she watched him over the hedge of green tongues, Nora felt proud of her Pelt. She grew fond of her hiding place and then, whenever she missed Pelt, she would come to hide in her green-tongued refuge. She was always happy when Pelt discovered her there and led her away. He scolded her gently on the way to the white room, where they brought her a pink pudding with a cherry on top, the A-1 lunch dessert of the day. Nora would eat the pink pudding with a cherry on top extremely slowly, in order to prolong as much as possible these moments when she had Pelt all to herself, and she would try to absorb the scent of his room, Pelt's scent. Not even when Pelt would come for brief visits to Babylon would the scent have faded away, Pelt's hair and sparse ashen beard exuded it.

Nora Paskal is convinced that if she could bend down over Pelt here in Strašnice, if the sharp green tongues and the glass partition were not in her way, she would again smell the old familiar scent. But Mrs Beaver-Pelt is also there, the one who stole Pelt from Nora years ago. And over there, hiding behind a column, is the mother of Nora Paskal and of four other unborn children (destroyed at Pelt's bidding), she is standing behind the column so as not to be seen by the second Mrs Pelt, but even more likely, she is hiding there so as not to be seen by Pelt. She surely has not forgotten, not even today, at least in spirit, to carefully rake the path Pelt will walk along to the gazebo, at least in spirit she must have sprinkled it with white sand, with sand as white as flour from the time of the First World War. Even today she must have baked pastries, just in case the funeral party from Strašnice would come to call. She would even offer some to the second Mrs Pelt, she feels no ill will toward her.

There lies Pelt, and as he lies there, his feet begin to feel cold, he is wearing only thin brown socks and it is cold in the Strašnice gazebo despite its being summertime. This year the summer has been strangely cold, thinks Pelt, experiments in the atmosphere are having an unfavourable influence on the weather, and also on the skin, on that too. Pelt can clearly see his dead daughter Nora standing beyond the glass partition and the green tongues, he can clearly see even his four unborn children standing there with her (one of them is a boy), he can also see family members who are still alive — grandson Diviš (he hasn't seen him since he was a child) and the clergyman Jan Paskal, the son-in-law, currently a dealer in animal skins. And of course he can also see Mrs Pelt, who caused his last Christmas tree to be stripped bare, who caused Pelt himself to be stripped bare as well. But most clearly of all he can see the first one, the one behind the column, her funereal shadow falls across his face and Pelt, in his final immobility, cannot shake it off. She has baked those pastries again, she most definitely has, to remind him of how he wronged his family, to overwhelm him with silent reproaches even now in the hour of his death. What luck to have the glass partition and the green tongues to separate them, what luck that she cannot hand him the pastries through the glass and over the sharp green tongues. Pelt rejoices in getting the best of her this time. But it's a pity there are no paradise trees anywhere, not a single one.

Only in the meadow behind the crematorium, after Pelt's fine grey ashes have been scattered and are mingling with the earth to be transformed into a new skin of life over the course of time, only then does Pelt realize the naïveté of his distaste for the pastries, he grasps the existence of a mysterious and fated cycle and sees the futility of resisting it. For, dear Pelt, whether you eat the pastry from paradise or not — either way, skin thou art, and unto skin shalt thou return.

THE NATION

I am the nation. I have fallen into Egyptian captivity once more. I profess the faith that receives the sacrament in both kinds, the body and the blood of the Lord. I have my own knaves and my own onion soup. I have my own revolutions and my own heroes. One of them burst into flames on a pyre he had built himself — between the National Museum and the Food Bazaar. Professor Pelt was called to him and saw an entire nation immersed in an oil bath, a nation flayed beyond any help, even beyond the help of the miraculous Professor Pelt.

I am the nation disillusioned by all its revolutions and its occupations, even by its sacrifices to fire. I am a nation that converted. I am Jan Paskal, clergyman of the Church of Bohemian Brethren, now dealing in feathers and animal skins of every description, a frequent guest in Bartholomew Street. I am Bartholomew Paskal — one cat skin. And I am also Diviš Paskal, a former student of ethnography, a thief of onions at the market in Havel Street. I am Alice Davidovič, ever searching for my sweetheart. I am Pavel Santner rummaging through shells on the seashore. I am a Mother-of-Pearl Queen at a charity ball. I am Nora Pelt-Paskal and I make love in a Babylonian gazebo right after the war. I am Vojtěch Paskal, the prodigal son. I am Mařenka Tůňka from a village near Blaník Mountain, seduced and abandoned, waiting at the foot of the mountain, waiting for it to open and return my hanged brother Jan. I am Mortar and I am Wildboar, the two flayers from Bartholomew Street.

I am Mr Köck miraculously transformed during the revolution, and I am Caretaker Briar pointing his finger. I am also Thomas Hamza, the doubting one who came to believe, the one who gave away his handkerchief and then regretted it. I am Nanynka Shmid, the girl so afraid of the ground. And I am Georgie Briar, the one with the pin. I am also Mr Turk and Mr Klečka and all the others at Olšany — Mr Havlíček, who has been taken to Brixen, and Mr Sabina, traitor of the nation. I am Grandfather and Grandmother Davidovič, for years I have been dwelling in the pantry, while Herr Hergesell haunts the lightwell.

I am the nation. I live in a flat across from the Olšany Cemetery, in a flat formerly of Jewish and then of German tenants. There the living cede ground to the dead who are growing too cramped in the pantry. The last living one, Diviš Paskal, will be torn to pieces like Dionysus and Orpheus, he is Diviš Zagreus, the one who discovered the world in the lightwell, or rather within himself. What audacity and what conceit! I am the new Davidovič, who was born and whose fate is already sealed.

But perhaps I am merely a bird, the Chamberlain, who sleeps upside down, or a rat, the Chambermaid, who gratefully rubs against the legs of those who feed her breadcrumbs.

GEORGIE BRIAR'S DESCENT

The imperial eagle Hergesell returns to the lightwell with the vernal winds. From time to time, Grandmother Davidovič can hear him rustling and always makes sure the little window is properly closed. But Benjamin, the youngest of the Davidovič line, is not there with him, for the eagle left him to die at Hagibor. He expected him to be torn to pieces by wild animals, but the child was found by Doe, the ball boy. What if he is a royal child, thinks Doe, not realizing how close he is to the truth. And what if one day this abandoned child will solve the riddle and drive the plague from this city? Doe is struck by the idea of bringing up the foundling to be a ball boy, his successor.

Caretaker Briar naturally doesn't fail to notice Hergesell's return. Let him stay, as long as no one lets him in. And he orders Georgie not to touch the lightwell window and, as a precaution, barricades the window with a wardrobe. Lately Caretaker Briar has begun to fear death and imagines that such fortifications will protect him from it.

Georgie Briar, as he sits on the sofa with his legs tucked under him day in and day out, keeps straining his ears and seems to hear a soft crying. What if Alice is crying in the lightwell for her lost muff because Diviš never gave it to her, deceiving both Georgie and Alice. And what if Alice thinks Georgie has the muff, she may have come to believe Diviš's lies and Georgie will never be able to explain to her that it happened quite otherwise, that he was keeping it for her all along, that he was waiting for her to come for it and sit next to him again, as she had before. And that he would then ceremoniously produce the muff, and Alice would place her hands in it and let Georgie do the same, and then Georgie Briar would rise from the sofa, no longer a child but a man, and take Alice for his wife. For the longer the muff lay untouched inside the sofa upon which Georgie Briar was enthroned, the more it was transformed in his imagination into a mysterious object of metamorphosis. And as soon as they both would touch it, they would be metamorphosed and the muff itself would also disappear, leaving a little black lamb bleating pitifully and trying to stand on its wobbly legs. And now it seemed to Georgie that it wasn't Alice crying in the lightwell but an abandoned little lamb, a little black Persian lamb who returns to Georgie but finds the gate shut.

And at that moment Georgie gets up from the sofa, goes to the pantry, pushes away the wardrobe, God only knows where he got the strength, and throws the little window wide open. He's calling Alice, his little lamb: Come home, you can come home now, Georgie Briar has opened the gate for you. But dead silence reigns in the lightwell, not a sound. The bleating must have tired the little lamb and now it has fallen asleep down there, Georgie surmises, leaning out as far as he can to look for the little animal. And as Georgie leans out and looks for the little lamb, he inhales the lightwell air, and the lightwell dust gets into his eyes and into his ears and into his nose. He strains to see the little lamb at the bottom of the lightwell. Perhaps one can't see the little animal because it's all black, he thinks. So Georgie decides to drop his legs in and jump down. It's closer to the bottom from here than from the fifth floor, since the caretaker's apartment is on the ground floor. And now Georgie Briar is standing at the very bottom. Behold the descent of Georgie Briar. Georgie doesn't know that he isn't the first one to undertake this journey, someone did so up above, and he down below. And if he knew that it was none other than Diviš Paskal, he would hate him even more.

Georgie gropes the floor around him with his hands, he's looking for the little Persian lamb but can't find it. And then he remembers Alice and calls out her name. Just then a little window upstairs opens and Georgie sees Alice. But it's no longer his Alice, this one is old and ugly. And the transformed Alice puts a finger to her lips, signalling Georgie Briar to be silent. Alice's head is encircled with a lightwell halo. And Georgie grows silent, huddles in a corner, drawing his legs up beneath him. And as flecks of lightwell dust settle on Georgie, as the flecks gradually cover him, Georgie slowly falls asleep. Georgie of the Lightwell is asleep now, his childlike dream filled with the sound of bleating lambs, he sees Alice, she is beautiful again and pours milk for the little lamb, now the little lamb bends down to the milk but suddenly the dish of milk overturns. Georgie and Alice try to stop the milk with their hands so the little lamb can drink, but the milk runs through their fingers, milk of transience, milk of death.

Suddenly out of nowhere, the eagle Hergesell alights at the bottom of the lightwell. As the eagle strikes the ground with his wings, the lightwell dust swirls up, the gust of air grazes the sleeper's cheek and he awakens. When Georgie sees Herr Hergesell standing before him, he realizes it was he who upset the lamb's dish of milk. Georgie searches for the pin in his pocket. But the pin is not in his pocket, Herr Hergesell has long since had the pin, Georgie should have guessed as much right away. At the bottom of the lightwell, Georgie stands up on his wobbly legs and sees the pin glistening in the lapel of Hergesell's coat. — Give the pin back to Georgie! But Herr Hergesell doesn't even stir, let alone move to give back the pin. At that moment Georgie sees it all: Hergesell knows everything about him, he also knows that he killed Alice Davidovič with the pin because she was holding hands with Pavel Santner and allowed him to carry her muff. And he knows that later on he stabbed Kostya Sukhoruchkov with the same pin because he pretended to be someone else, and Georgie wanted to stab him again for having renounced him. But Herr Hergesell probably suspects that if he gave Georgie back the pin, Georgie would stab him with it too, for having overturned the lamb's dish of milk. He would also stab Diviš Paskal, because he had deceived Georgie and tricked him out of the muff. Suddenly Georgie sees that it isn't Herr Hergesell but a wolf, and he cries out for help. All the lightwell windows open up one after another and everyone can see Georgie at the bottom of the lightwell.

Later on, when Georgie is hauled out of the wolf's den and carried off to the bathtub, all along the way he scatters the lightwell dust, the dust of the knowledge of life and death. And Caretaker Briar suddenly notices Herr Hergesell striding along the black path behind Georgie, the one whose resurrection he had so feared and against whom he had put up the wardrobe in the pantry. Herr Hergesell sits down on the sofa next to Georgie after his bath, the pin glistening in the lapel of his coat.

— What smells so bad in here, Briar? That is exactly what Caretaker Briar feared. — Cabbage, Herr Hergesell, nice sweet cabbage. — You're a liar, Briar. It's American chocolate, iodine, Russian tobacco. And right after that Herr Hergesell wants to see the record book. Caretaker Briar insists he hasn't kept one for a long time. But Herr Hergesell pulls out the record book himself and immediately observes that his request for a new bathtub has disappeared from it. And that means trouble for the caretaker.

— There was a muff here, where did you hide it, Briar? At that moment Georgie on the sofa gives a start, why they're talking about the Persian lamb. So his father had it too? Herr Hergesell points his finger at the sofa, right at the spot where Georgie Briar is sitting. — It was there, there, for all these thirty years. The father and the son look at each other. So he also had the muff, Georgie thinks, and begins to feel hatred for his father. And if he had his pin, he would stab his father now as well.

— And what about Mr Klečka and Mr Turk, such nice gentlemen, what happened to them? Briar doesn't know, Briar doesn't remember, he doesn't know anything about the clergyman upstairs either, except that he hasn't been preaching for many years. Briar begs, pleads, uses his son as an excuse: He's still a child and will always remain a child, such a misfortune. And you'll get your bathtub, Herr Hergesell, a nice new one, you'll take a bath and at once you'll feel reborn…

Georgie Briar is sitting on the sofa, his legs tucked under him, precisely over the place where for almost thirty years Alice Davidovič's muff used to lie, the little Persian lamb cursed into the likeness of a muff. They've slaughtered Georgie's little lamb. Georgie can see a trickle of its blood seeping out from under the sofa and mingling in the middle of the kitchen with a trickle of milk. He watches the pink puddle and then jumps up on his wobbly legs, he wants to catch the lamb's blood and the milk in his hands, but the lamb's blood and the milk run through his fingers. Thus Georgie, Georgie Briar, the one who descended to the bottom of the lightwell, comes to know death in a pink flow in the middle of the kitchen. What if Georgie were to sprinkle the dead lamb with Bubeník's living water, would it not then return to life?

On warm evenings the cemetery virgins come to bathe in the Olšany pond, they don't mind that the water is dirty and barely reaches their knees. Alice Davidovič is not among them and neither is Nanynka Shmid, she is afraid of water. And Pavel Santner, seeing that Alice Davidovič isn't bathing in the pond, goes for a stroll along the bank. It reminds him of the Côte d'Azur, and he keeps looking for shells even here — *Heliotis* shells and *Iris* shells, *Nautilus pompilius* shells and *Turbo olearius* shells, and one shell by the name of *Strombus gigas*. And then something extraordinary happens — Pavel Santner finds a button, a button of mother-of-pearl, with two holes. He picks up the button and examines it in disbelief. He ponders whether the button is made of Manila mother-of-pearl, or if it is the Makassar variety, or if it isn't actually Kikeriki, which has become quite rare.

The button lies in the palm of Pavel Santner's hand, evoking a multitude of memories and countless images. So immersed is he in reminiscing that he doesn't even notice Mr Šafařík. Mr Šafařík is profoundly depressed, among other reasons because he has learned that Sabina frequents the Bartholomew Street headquarters, and that Havlíček has been taken to Brixen again. It was truly naïve of Mr Šafařík to believe the rule of bayonets and spies was going to its grave. Mr Šafařík has a feeling that those two thugs are at his heels all the time, and whom can one trust, whom? And then there is the pain, the intense pain in his right leg, spreading from his big toe along his instep and then upward.

Mr Šafařík must be thinking he's under the Francis Bridge when he jumps into the Olšany pond. The splash rouses Pavel Santner from his contemplation of the mother-of-pearl button and he rushes to Mr Šafařík's rescue. How is he supposed to know that it's not an accident, that it's Mr Šafařík's second attempt on his own life — his own death, as a matter of fact. Good Lord, is this Mr Šafařík? This pitiful shrivelled old man, now sodden with water, wonders Pavel Santner as he carries Mr Šafařík out of the

Olšany pond, while clenching the button in his teeth. Should Mr Kollár once again ask what will have become of us, the Slavs, a hundred years from now, I will point to Mr Šafařík, who went to drown himself in a pond where the water barely reached his knees, but he couldn't have known.

Mr Šafařík is shivering all over — with cold, yes, but above all with fear. And at the same time, Mr Šafařík feels ashamed, deeply ashamed, for not having drowned himself and for having mistaken the Olšany pond for the Vltava River. But no, he hasn't mistaken one for the other, he simply couldn't go any farther, that's what happened. And what will Božena Julie Ambrosy say, and the children, what will they say? And Mr Šafařík begs Pavel Santner to leave him there by the wall, he'll go on alone as soon as he dries off a little, and no, he won't go back to the river. So he does think it was a river instead of a pond, everything gets muddled in his head. — They don't know what shame is, says Mr Šafařík after Pavel Santner has set him down by the wall. Pavel Santner knows very well what shame is, take for instance the time he and Alice Davidovič lay in the sparse grass full of dog faeces at the top of Gallows Hill. He's been avoiding Alice ever since. But he can't tell this to Mr Šafařík. He takes the button out of his mouth and shows it to Mr Šafařík to distract him a little. — Look, I found a button there by the pond, it's a nice one, made of mother-of-pearl. It's most likely Manila or Makassar mother-of-pearl, or perhaps, who knows, Kikeriki mother-of-pearl.

Mr Šafařík listens to Pavel Santner telling him about mother-of-pearl, it seems quite natural since Pavel Santner used to be a seashell merchant. And as Pavel Santner talks, Mr Šafařík listens and slowly dries off, by now Mr Šafařík is almost completely dry, soon he'll be able to return to his loved ones, to his domestic paradise, as he used to call it. Mr Šafařík sets out at a slow pace, his right leg slightly lame, and turns back once more to wave at Pavel Santner.

Once Mr Šafařík has disappeared from sight, Pavel Santner examines the button more carefully and discovers tiny black spots on its shiny surface, the Kikeriki mother-of-pearl was probably eaten through by parasites. How come he didn't notice this right away at the pond and sees it only now? The pond is probably full of such useless shells. And only now does Pavel Santner begin to understand how Mr Šafařík must feel: to him the world looks just like this button — all aglitter, but when you examine it more closely and from a different angle, you see that its mother-of-pearl is flawed, that it's simply a reject. And Pavel Santner, the seashell merchant, throws the button as far away as he can. And suddenly he feels a sense of relief, as if he had been holding the whole contaminated world in his teeth.

Pavel Santner, the seashell merchant, doesn't know that Nora Pelt sees him. Nora watches Pavel Santner throw away the button, and no sooner is he gone, she scours the place where he threw it. She's been here for a while and has overheard the whole conversation between the two men. She was especially intrigued by Santner's talk about mother-of-pearl. It reminded her of something from the distant past, of a house where heaps of shells were sliding and collapsing and softly rattling. From somewhere there even emerged the shadow of her grandmother bending over Nora, a shell in her hair, and from that shell the sound of the Chrudimka stream murmured in Nora's ears.

Nora picks up the button and at that moment her memories become much clearer, in fact they are so clear that they materialize before her eyes like frozen images, Nora can enter them at will or, rather, can find herself in them, because she too has been frozen in those images, enchanted within them. Just the slightest turn of the button, and suddenly Nora is in one of them: she's eating a pink pudding with a cherry on top and Pelt is talking... Nora turns the button a bit more, she's not exactly in the mood to hear about leprosy, which one sees everywhere, anywhere one looks. And at once she is somewhere else entirely: she's sitting on a white wicker chair in Babylon, and Pelt... She turns the button again and suddenly that strange scent wafts over her, she

126

doesn't know it's the scent of Kain — Paskal lays his head in her lap, as the sacred unicorn lays his head in the lap of a virgin, no longer a virgin.

Had Pavel Santner had an inkling of the button's powers, he would hardly have rid himself of it so casually. Yet perhaps Pavel Santner did know, but he was not in a mood for reminiscing. Afterwards one is overwhelmed by anxiety, such anxiety. Nora Paskal feels anxious too, she misses Diviš, it is hard to be so close to one's son and at the same time so far away. But should Nora overstep the boundary, things would go badly for Diviš. Yet what is good and what is bad? The mother-of-pearl button glistens in the moonlight, and Nora Paskal realizes it's a button of temptation. She knows she'll hardly be able to resist temptation, in fact the thought of it excites her, she longs to succumb to temptation at least for a moment, to wrench herself from the plague torpor reigning all around, to flirt a little with the serpent.

And Nora turns over the button. In that moment the serpent coils around her body, but it isn't a serpent, it's a wolf, it isn't a wolf, it's Herr Hergesell from the fifth floor. He addresses her as Frau Lamm, which somewhat translates her last name, her paschal name. And since it happens to be Shrovetide before Easter, Herr Hergesell begs an angel wing from Nora — they used to bake these crispy pastries in her grandmother's house, they simply melted in one's mouth. But Herr Hergesell is hardly thinking of Shrovetide pastries. And Nora Paskal finds his pre-Easter blasphemy exciting.

If only her anxiety were not becoming more and more unbearable. If only the core of the apple Nora Paskal has sunk her teeth into by mistake were not so bitter. If only the reverse side of the mother-of-pearl button were not speckled with tiny black spots left behind by parasites, something Nora Paskal hadn't noticed. Nevertheless Nora is going to keep the button, for it offers one the possibility of rediscovering the whole world, the entire lost paradise, a slight turn this way or that, and everything abruptly changes. And even the bitterness, even the nostalgia, even the anxiety is better than the plague torpor, much better.

What is this new business of Diviš's all about, why is he saying there never was a child, that supposedly no one has ever seen a little Benjamin Davidovič, and for that matter, why should he be called Davidovič to begin with, and not Santner after his father — Benjamin Santner, since Alice claims he is the child of their love? It is with these words that Diviš assaults Alice just as she has finished her climb up the hill alongside the cemetery wall. He planned it well, calculating that Alice, out of breath, would slow down and thus have to hear him out. However Diviš doesn't know that Alice and Pavel Santner have already met, and that she is no longer in a hurry because she has realized that Pavel Santner isn't coming to ask Grandfather Davidovič for her hand, definitely not now. And she also knows he probably would not have come then, even had he not left with a transport.

No one but Alice knows what went on when Pavel Santner was leaving, and Diviš has no right to put into words something she hasn't admitted to herself all these years. But isn't Alice behaving the same way when she talks to Diviš, aren't her words equally harsh, don't they cut to the quick? What if it was true that Alice Davidovič used to run after Pavel Santner like a black sheep, and he would occasionally take her to the top of Gallows Hill only out of pity? And since he didn't know what to do with his hands, he would play with her muff. A lover's embrace, a soft lap — maybe none of that ever was. Instead, just some desiccated caresses, desiccated like the dog faeces in the sparse grass. So, perhaps, was Alice Davidovič's immaculate conception on top of Gallows Hill, from which a new Davidovič was to be born, from this conception-nonconception. And where, indeed, is Benjamin, where has the child gone?

Alice Davidovič turns away from Diviš but doesn't try to run from him, she has no strength left. What right does he have, he who beguiled his way into their midst, to judge her love, what right? And just then Diviš snatches away her Sabbath tablecloth and out falls — not Benjamin Davidovič but the muff made of a little Persian lamb still unborn. And who gave her back the muff, who? Diviš reminds Alice of his service, hoping she'll relent.

As Alice stops at the threshold of the house, her hands hidden in the muff, Georgie runs out. Before he can utter his pleas, she hands him the muff and goes away, without even looking back. Georgie stands there helpless, slips first one hand, then the other, inside the muff, but feels nothing, no rapture as before. Disappointed, he throws the muff away. And Caretaker Briar picks up the muff, it's still nice, it's Persian lamb. And maybe Alice is lying on the sidewalk again, but no one can see her now, no one except those who are themselves dead or nearing death. And in the evening, when Mr Klečka comes again to see Mr Turk in the tomb, the latter says: Everything repeats itself, only each time in a slightly different way, a worse way.

All is quiet at the Olšany Cemetery. The peace is disturbed only occasionally by squirrels scattering in all directions before Horngoat and Hoardgold. It's too bad they can't see how many servile Olšany residents are surrounding them, crowding in on them, every one of them pointing at something, even at one another. But Horngoat and Hoardgold take it to be the sound of old trees murmuring in the wind, they are not quite near enough to death to understand, although they're near enough to chase after the spectre of Mr Sabina, who gave them the slip in Bartholomew Street.

On one of the deserted paths, Mrs Havlíček prostrates herself at Horngoat's feet: I beg you, please let me go to Havlíček in Brixen. Mrs Havlíček must have mistaken Horngoat for Commissioner Dedera. But Horngoat-Dedera doesn't stop, maybe he hasn't even heard Mrs Havlíček, or else thinks she is one of the loonies always found in abundance at cemeteries. And Mrs Havlíček immediately regrets having humiliated herself. If only she were as strong as Alice Davidovič! And as soon as she thinks that, Alice Davidovič appears at her side and helps her get up.

— Mrs Havlíček, you shouldn't have done that. These people

will never take pity on anyone, never. But that's easy for Alice to say when all she has to do is climb up Gallows Hill. Alice just sighs. Another's misfortune always seems more bearable than one's own. Alice Davidovič doesn't have to go all the way to Brixen, it's true, but she would gladly go, gladly wear out seven pairs of shoes. Yes, all she has to do is climb up Gallows Hill, yet she carries her Brixen with her all the time, Brixen is always everywhere around her and even inside her, Alice feels the Tyrolean exile in the same place where she had carried Benjamin, the unconceived one of the Davidovič line, the place that now gapes empty. But everyone is too much alone, too much isolated in his own grief to be able to understand the grief of others.

THE POSTHUMOUS WOLF CUB

Jan Paskal — the lamb who bit through the wolf's neck, Abel who killed Cain in a flat across from the Olšany Cemetery. In the flat there is a pantry, in the pantry a wardrobe, in the wardrobe a skin. Whose skin is it? It is the skin of the lamb who soiled his hands with the blood of the wolf. But is it still a lamb if it disemboweled a wolf, hasn't the lamb thereby turned into a wolf? Or rather, and more likely, it is half-lamb and half-wolf. And just as in the fable, this strange creature settles down in the wolf's den. Why shouldn't he, when even Caretaker Briar is advising him to do so, why shouldn't he exchange his small flat for a larger one, especially since killing wolves is considered to be meritorious, not a sin? Yet there still exists a little Babylonian sheep that caused the lamb to attack the wolf...

But who is to believe this fable? Definitely not Vojtěch Paskal. The prodigal son has already met several times with two gentlemen at the Little Bears tavern, with Mr Horngoat and Mr Hoardgold, whom else. The two gentlemen fully understand Vojtěch's feelings, having a stepmother is hard, having been turned out of one's home is hard too. And even worse is having a weakling for a father, one who won't stand up for his first born. That the lamb devoured the wolf? Horngoat and Hoardgold are laughing. — Who has ever seen such a thing? Don't believe it, Vojtěch! — But who then? At the Little Bears, Horngoat and Hoardgold tell Vojtěch the story of Judith and Holofernes. Messrs Horngoat and Hoardgold whisper into Vojtěch's ear: Vojtěch, your little brother Diviš is a bastard. Has it never struck you how little you resemble one another, how little you understand each other?

From the Little Bears, Vojtěch Paskal goes directly to Olšany. Look, the prodigal son is returning, but instead of humility in his heart, he brings accusations to throw in his father's face. — You allowed your own blood to be driven away from home by a murderess, a harlot, and you coddle a wolf cub at your breast. Jan Paskal is silent, he says nothing, only the hands resting on his knees twitch every so often like two half-dead little animals being skinned alive. Jan Paskal doesn't answer, he is wondering who could have revealed these things to Vojtěch, things he always worried might be brought into the open one day. Who told him that Jan Paskal did not kill, that he was unable to kill, that he just raised his arm and inflicted a wound, that he did not deal the mortal blow. But the rest of it, the part about Diviš not being his son, that the German, Hergesell… — That's malicious gossip, Vojtěch, who told you that?

But Vojtěch Paskal doesn't believe his father. Even if his father had killed a fatted calf, he wouldn't believe him. — Diviš is a wolf, a posthumous wolf cub. And in Bartholomew Street they know this, too. — So that's it, that's where you got it from, don't you understand they'll use anything to turn you against me?

The posthumous wolf cub is sitting in the pantry but hears it all. Abruptly he opens the window onto the lightwell, not, however, because he wants to descend into it once more and feel the world within himself, but because he wants to ask Hergesell himself, that is if a dead man can answer such a question. But Grandmother Davidovič slams the window shut again: One shouldn't tempt fate, she says. Diviš agonizes over the uncertainty: Diviš Paskal or Diviš Hergesell, son of lamb or son of wolf, wheat or chaff, son of chaff? Who will now decide? Diviš is spread-eagled between two voids, one is sitting in the room resting with his hands on his knees, the other is in the lightwell, one terrifies him as much as the other, and he feels both equally within him.

TO BE, OR NOT TO BE

Georgie Briar is sitting on the sofa with his legs tucked under him. To be, or not to be? Should he go on sitting here, or seize the pin? Oh, to sleep — no more — and to know that the sleep will end the heartache, the grief that the body is heir to, oh, the body of an eternal child. To sleep — perchance to dream. But what if Georgie were to dream again about the slaughtered Persian lamb and thus rid himself of his body, his eternal child's body?

And suddenly Alice Davidovič is here, asking Georgie how he is. Earlier she would never have asked, it's only now, after seeing him in the lightwell and after Georgie saw Alice in there too. How can Georgie be, just let her step into his shoes for a moment. And Georgie tells Alice: Georgie wanted your muff, Alice, wanted it very badly. And the muff has turned into a little lamb. — Georgie, where is the little lamb? — You are the little lamb, Alice. The wolf ate the lamb. And Georgie bares his teeth at Alice.

Naturally Alice knows all this, she is just putting Georgie to the test. She is testing him to see whether she can use him for her plan. And she casually suggests to Georgie that they go for a soda at Bubeník's. And Georgie muses: So that's how it is, now Georgie is good enough for her. The little lamb desires living water. But who knows what might happen then. Perhaps she might then leave for good with Pavel Santner. Or perhaps with Diviš Paskal? And Georgie shakes his head, no, there won't be any water. There won't be any metamorphosis either, which is what Alice had been hoping for, and what Georgie was to help her achieve.

Alice… get thee to a cemetery!

Alice, the rejected little lamb, goes, hardly able to drag her feet. So Georgie too has deserted her, not even he will give her a drink of living water, not even he. No, Alice will not go to the cemetery, not there, she would end up like Nanynka Shmid or like Mrs Havlíček, soon she wouldn't be able to take even a single step. Or else she might begin to see the cemetery as a garden of delights — like Mr Klečka. No, Alice will not go to the cemetery for anything in the world, she will never call it home. She hates the perpetual milling of its crowd, the pestilential stench, the sweet languidness, the torpor so difficult to elude. She will not even go to meet Pavel Santner. What ecstasy he fell into from a mere button, a common ordinary button he found on the bank of the Olšany pond! Is this Pavel Santner, the Pavel Santner for whom she has been waiting all these years? Who then freed himself from her embrace on top of Gallows Hill, got up and brushed off his clothing, the longed-for bridegroom. Nor will she drown herself in the pond because of him, nor lose her mind. If only Georgie Briar hadn't grown so embittered. If only she did not long so to drink of the water she had earlier scorned, one little sip would suffice, then maybe everything might change at a stroke.

THE COMING OF BENJAMIN

Just as Alice Davidovič carried Benjamin, the youngest of the Davidovič line, not for nine months but for more than two decades, thus, conversely, the newborn Benjamin grew into a youth within several months. The reputation of his grace and kindness spread quickly and soon even crossed over the wall of the Olšany Cemetery, from where it wasn't far to Hagibor. And Nanynka Shmid, who is still holding Thomas Hamza's handkerchief and guarding it like a treasure, has a great desire to see Benjamin. She arranges with Mr Klečka to go to Hagibor to take a look at Benjamin, so they join hands and set out on their way. And Mr Turk looks after them with sadness because he knows what this means, but being wise he doesn't try to stop them. And the melancholy angel knows it too, and his head tilts even more to one side, because he has grown fond of Mr Klečka.

And now Nanynka Shmid and Mr Klečka are looking at the graceful Benjamin, they observe how swiftly and with what charm he picks up the tennis balls. And Benjamin notices Nanynka and Mr Klečka and feels so close to them that they could be his siblings. So transfixed is he by looking at them that he forgets to pick up the tennis balls, in vain do the players keep shouting at him, in vain does Doe try to reason with him through the fence.

And now Benjamin is standing there with Nanynka and Mr Klečka, and Nanynka hands him Thomas Hamza's silk handkerchief to wipe the sweat off his face. And after Benjamin wipes off his face with the handkerchief and hands it back to Nanynka, she sees that Benjamin's image is impressed upon it. And Mr Klečka, also seeing what a miracle has come to pass, at once forgets Mr Turk and walks along beside the graceful Benjamin as if in a trance. As they approach the cemetery, Benjamin hurries his steps, nearly flying through the air, drawn by the force of the place he doesn't yet know, and Nanynka Shmid and Mr Klečka can barely keep up with him.

Benjamin thinks to himself: How astonishing, just a moment ago I believed there was nothing more beautiful than picking up tennis balls and being with my father, that there was no more promised land than Hagibor, and then suddenly, the moment I saw these two behind the fence, everything changed, I have to follow them where they lead me and know that my proper place is precisely there, that my whole life up to now has been just a senseless groping. How astonishing, just a moment ago I was convinced that Doe from Vršovice was my father and I honoured and loved him like a father, and now I know that my father is someone else.

And as the three of them are nearing the cemetery, they meet a funeral procession, Thomas Hamza is being laid to rest. So his time, too, has come. And suddenly Thomas Hamza spots his lost handkerchief, the silk handkerchief with which his prolonged illness began, and reaches for it. But Nanynka holds the handkerchief tightly, for Benjamin's likeness is on it. But by now the handkerchief is threadbare — many a winter has passed over it, many a rain has soaked through it — and it tears, right down the middle. And Benjamin touches his face and his lips contort in pain. And Thomas Hamza, seeing what he has caused, feels remorse, but there's nothing to be done about it any more. And Benjamin's face, which up to now has been graced with a charming smile, grows sombre and assumes the expression of the wounded melancholy angel. And Mr Klečka, catching Nanynka about to collapse, says to Thomas Hamza: See what you've done. Thomas Hamza tries to explain that it is, after all, his handkerchief, but the other three are no longer listening to him, they are leaving, meanwhile the mourners begin to throw handfuls of earth on Thomas Hamza. One clump falls on the shred of the silk handkerchief, on the face of Benjamin Davidovič, impressed upon it and rent in two. And coming at the very onset of Benjamin's kingdom, this did not bode well.

THE LEPER KING

It was not only Thomas Hamza's silk handkerchief that turned out to be too fine and threadbare, and so tore in half, but also the face of Benjamin, the youngest of the Davidovič line, the little lamb never born, that face was also too fine and threadbare. The rending of its impression on the handkerchief sufficed to distort its integrity, the face began to fade like a too long cherished dream. It was fading right before the eyes of Nanynka Shmid and Mr Klečka. And the part Thomas Hamza had taken with him into his grave, impressed on a shred of the handkerchief, that part especially was undergoing a change. Thomas Hamza, always so exceedingly prudent and indecisive, had brought about such a misfortune for the sake of a piece of silk, he of all people, a man from whom such an act of brutality could hardly have been expected.

Benjamin's face tilts to one side. Nanynka recognizes the face — it's the face of the melancholy angel. Every so often Nanynka presses against it the remnant of silk. Mr Klečka, however, has turned away, he doesn't have the courage to look at the transformed face whose grace he had earlier followed as if entranced.

And then an old man appears next to them, for a long time his eyes scrutinize Benjamin's face, the face of a fading dream. — Most strange. I haven't seen such a case in a long time. This is Hansen's disease, otherwise called leprosy. It is caused by Hansen's bacillus. (Hasn't the gentleman made a mistake, doesn't he mean Hamza's bacillus? thinks Nanynka Shmid.) It is, of course, Doctor Pelt, who else, he is the one giving the present talk on skin, on Benjamin's skin, on the skin of a disintegrating dream. — Look, a classic case of leonine facies, Doctor Pelt still manages to say before Nora claps her hand over his mouth. She's fed up with his endless lectures on skin, with the carapace of words that has been suffocating her since childhood and through which his gaze could never really reach her. Pelt has been silenced, but of what use is it, almost everyone has heard him and now they are slowly assembling, staring with curiosity at the leonine visage, and some of them then step back in horror. Pelt would like to explain to them that Hansen's (Hamza's, according to Nanynka) bacillus is not as dangerous as was once believed, that it requires a favourable breeding ground (yet isn't the Olšany earth precisely the most favourable ground of all?) and that the probability of contagion is relatively low, but Nora has already taken him by the hand and is leading him away.

And at that moment someone notices that Benjamin is accompanied by Nanynka Shmid, the one who once held the traitor of the nation's hat, and by Mr Klečka, who lives with Mr Turk (an odd man, that one) — that in itself works against Benjamin. Is this supposed to be the king of Olšany, the graceful youth they have been waiting for all this time and who was supposed to bring them salvation? Where has his grace gone, and his smile, where has his face gone? And everyone around grumbles, and some of them even raise their fists because they feel betrayed. And what if it isn't leprosy after all but the plague, the chronic plague that will carry them all away? But to where, to where else, aren't they already down far enough, the lowest one can go? Who knows?

Mr Klečka suddenly gets up and slowly walks away, stepping over the graves as though moonstruck. He picks graveyard flowers as he goes. And Mr Turk, watching him, realizes that Mr Klečka has just lost his mind, and this makes him sad. Nanynka Shmid realizes this as well, her hand holding the remnant of the handkerchief falls listless into her lap, she has stopped wiping Benjamin's face, or rather what is left of his face, what can she do against Hamza's bacillus? And when Benjamin sends her away because he wants to be alone, she obediently gets up and goes. And Benjamin is left alone in the Olšany lowlands, the redeemer deserted by all, denied by all, the lamb with a leonine face, the leper king of the graveyard's making.

Mr Klečka is wandering around the cemetery, picking graveyard flowers and also graveyard grass. — The couch grass is for you, Mr Sabina, and the panic grass here for Mr Šafařík. And then, as Mr Klečka sees Nanynka Shmid, he hands her a flower too. — I've been saving the milkwort for Nanynka. Here, Nanynka, take it. Nanynka would rather not take the milkwort, the name reminds her of something very sad in her life, a milky trickle, but still she takes the milkwort, so as not to sadden Mr Klečka. Mr Turk alone has not yet been given a flower, perhaps because Mr Klečka would like to pick him some bitterroot or bitterweed, but neither grows at Olšany, or because Mr Klečka has simply forgotten all about Mr Turk.

As Mr Klečka hands out graveyard flowers and also graveyard grass, no one even notices that Benjamin is no longer there. Maybe he has returned to Hagibor, from where he came. Or perhaps, just as his face disappeared, all of him has gradually disappeared, dissolved into the Olšany dusk. And maybe there never even was a Benjamin and it was all just Alice Davidovič's dream, about her expecting Pavel Santner's child, an Olšany dream taken for real. Yet there was, after all, the image, the disquieting face impressed upon Thomas Hamza's handkerchief. Who knows what would have happened had Thomas Hamza not torn it in two? But how was he to foresee the outcome, when all he wanted was to get back his handkerchief?

Alice Davidovič stands by the cemetery wall, wailing. Mr Turk comes out of his tomb and weeps with her. He has known for a long time that it would come to this, he has known how dangerous it is to dream, especially here, in this pestilential captivity. No one can ever be sure how a dream will be fulfilled, a dream seldom gives rise to anything good. One need only look at Alice Davidovič or Mr Klečka.

And what about Nanynka Shmid? They snatched from her the remnant of the handkerchief with Benjamin's face on it, that last remembrance and proof of his existence, they tore it up into shreds that are still fluttering about the cemetery. Benjamin Zagreus — Benjamin, the Lacerated one. And Nanynka Shmid is crying for him, Benjamin was but is no longer. She is all the more sad because the summer is coming to an end, the Shmids are leaving, and Nanynka will be left alone down here for a whole year, completely alone, and she is so afraid of the ground, now even more than before.

THE PUPPETS

Puppets are floating in the foul-smelling Botič stream. Claudia Glaire, who is walking home along the Botič, finds this odd, she longs for the puppets and steps into the water, what does it matter that it's December. The water only comes up to Claudia's knees. The puppets' bodies are short and their heads disproportionately large. Before long Claudia has collected an armful of puppets. The waterlogged wood of the puppets exudes a smell that makes Claudia dizzy. One of the puppets represents a king, but the features of the royal face are blurred, the water of the Botič must have dissolved them.

Claudia is stealing home with the puppets hidden under her coat, she hurries to avoid being seen by Randy and Slash, those two would hardly appreciate puppets pulled from a stream, they certainly would not, they have no appreciation for any of Claudia's games except the one where she strides along the ramparts, since there they have the roles of the executioner's knaves. Claudia need only stop for a moment in front of the theatrical supplies store in Bartholomew Street, and already they are on her, pushing her to move along. She'd better not look at all that stuff, she'll only make herself miserable for no reason and yield to all sorts of fantasies, remember the theatre didn't want her, her talent wasn't good enough for the stage. One day she'll come to realize that making black coffee for Bartošek is preferable by far, she must come to realize that one day, and it had better be soon.

Claudia has her own idea about all this. Why on earth does she hang out with these two? Because once, long ago, in Mrač, she let them dust her off when she was all white with flour from her loaves of bread, and by touching her Randy and Slash had cast a spell on her, although back then she had suspected nothing (didn't Diviš Paskal dust her off once, too?). As Claudia now holds the puppets in her arms (the king with blurred features among them), she finds the two men with their worldly wisdom and their servile zeal even more intolerable. And as Claudia holds the waterlogged puppets and inhales their Botič scent, she suddenly feels bold enough to rid herself of those two, to run away from them, even as far as the end of the earth, perhaps they won't follow her that far.

However, as Claudia hurries home contemplating her escape, those two are at her heels again, with no appreciation for any games, except perhaps for the one in Bartholomew Street. And Randy and Slash quickly take the puppets away from Claudia, one after another, and throw them, including the king, back into the Botič. What's the use of such puppets, and besides, they stink of that water, can't Claudia smell it? It's time to stop playing games, when will Claudia finally come to her senses, when will she become reasonable?

And while listening to Randy and Slash and watching the puppets being carried away by the water, one by one, even the king with blurred features, Claudia suddenly begins to realize she can never escape from them, those two will be lurking at the end of every dream, always ready to explain how childishly she has behaved, how tying Och's shoe laces is more laudable than haunting the ramparts, how making black coffee for Bartošek is more meritorious than staring at a theatrical supplies store. By the time Claudia Glaire loses sight of the puppets, as the water has carried them away, she no longer even doubts that it's better for her like this, her talent wasn't good enough for the stage anyway. Perhaps there never even were any puppets, how would they have got into the Botič, and how nastily the stream stinks, she must have dreamt it all. She is only surprised that her feet are wet and those two are carefully drying them.

THE BARTHOLOMEW PASS

Claudia the White Lady is wandering along Bartholomew Street. If Diviš Paskal could see her, he would certainly call to her: Watch out, Claudia, don't fall! But where could Claudia fall? Claudia is not afraid of the ground, she isn't even afraid of Bartholomew Street, she isn't like Nanynka Shmid, although she resembles Nanynka because she used to walk the ramparts of the town of Vertebra, while Nanynka Shmid learned to walk the tightrope. And now the two Bartholomew knaves, Randy and Slash, have seized Claudia. Again she was standing in front of the theatrical supplies store. Now the two Bartholomew knaves are leading her across the street to Major Bartošek to make him black coffee and tie his shoelaces. Now white Claudia is making black coffee for Bartošek and tying his shoelaces in Bartholomew Street.

Randy and Slash go to fetch Diviš: Come along with us, Diviš, to Bartholomew Street! Claudia is with Bartošek, who can get her away from there if not you? Diviš doesn't see through the ruse, he feels the time has come to turn somersaults before Bartošek, the time has come to crawl into the pass. If only it weren't again the Bartholomew Pass, where he must scrape off his skin for Claudia's sake. Is Claudia really still so white? Yet how many before him have descended to her and how many have come back? Could he be the chosen one?

And Diviš Paskal feels like Hercules, like Theseus, like Orpheus, and like Christ, and also like the poet Dante — this smugness will prove fatal to him. Diviš doesn't suspect that it's just a trap set for him by the hunters, Diviš the unicorn is about to put his head in the lap of a virgin, into a Bartholomew lap. Ring a ring o' roses — when you enter the pass you will lose your head fast, whoever you may be, fiddle-dee-dee. Hasn't Diviš considered at all that even if someone should return from there, he'll no longer be the same? And even if he doesn't touch any forbidden food, inhaling the Bartholomew air will be enough. He already feels faint from the air, just like his father when he had come this way.

In one room where Randy and Slash take Diviš, there's a wheel turning. Isn't that the wheel from Hagibor, and isn't Grandfather Davidovič still bound to it? And in another room there's a kind of monster, half human and half beast, a man with a skin-coat pulled over his head. Two men are leading him around the room: Blind man, guess where we're taking you? And Diviš recognizes Horngoat and Hoardgold. And the man wrapped in the skin, or rather in the coat, answers: To hell. And Diviš Paskal recoils because he recognizes his father.

And then Slash and Randy take Diviš up a staircase, up a winding staircase, like the one in the lookout tower on Petřín Hill. And who knows why it occurs to Diviš that he is going to see the starry sky up there, with Nanynka Shmid floating along the Milky Way. Only it's not Nanynka Shmid who's there but Claudia Glaire. She's walking on the Bartholomew ramparts, munching almonds.

Does Claudia really think Diviš is going to plead for her, that he'll crawl through some pass again? It was naïve of him even then, now he knows for sure, Claudia probably quite liked pouring wine for Och and tying the laces of his trainers. And should Diviš make it through the pass and thus enable her to return to the ramparts, she would hold it against him in the end. And what about the pass in Nusle, by the Botič stream, where the same two, Randy and Slash, were waiting on the other side? And Diviš suddenly understands: whether he makes it through the pass or not, they will always be waiting there — the plague knaves. And what will Diviš turn into when he finds himself between them, like his father between Horngoat and Hoardgold? He will then be the third man, he will don a jester's cap without noticing that it's really a knave's cap and will descend into the lap of Claudia, the Bartholomew harlot. Even in that way he is like the other two, even in that way. For by what right does Diviš presume to be different from them when he takes part in their game? Where is the boundary between the Bartholomew game and life?

They leave him alone with Claudia, saying they'll just drop by the Little Bears for a beer, for a beer or two. Claudia holds a handful of almonds, munching one after another, she offers some to Diviš too. As if Diviš didn't know he mustn't touch any thing here if he ever wants to get away. Diviš takes an almond from Claudia and eats it. And as soon as the bitter taste of the Bartholomew almond dissolves on his tongue, Diviš recoils, but it's already too late. By then Claudia is sitting in his lap. Diviš, who has eaten the almond of knowledge, now for the third time has entered a pass, the Bartholomew Pass. And as he tries to go back, his way is blocked by those two, Randy and Slash, already back from the Little Bears.

According to the numerical cabala of Agrippa of Nettesheim, if the integer one is the source and origin of all numbers, excluding all plurality, remaining always the same and constant, resulting in itself when multiplied by itself, having no beginning and relating to God, then the integer two, which immediately follows it, is the number of creation, the manifestation of primary motion. All incarnation proceeds from the integer two, the integer that is the principle of division, of plurality and of differentiation, of matter and of metamorphosis, it is the integer of science, of memory and of the world, of man, of discord and of impurity. According to the same Agrippa of Nettesheim, it is precisely the number two that gives rise to all nocturnal apparitions, nightmares and ghosts. It is the most favourable number for divination. The Pythagoreans considered the integer two an evil demon. Some do not even deem it a number, but rather a mere distortion of the integer one. On Mount Sinai there were two tablets of the law, in Exodus two cherubim gazed toward the mercy seat of the Tabernacle, in Zechariah's vision two olive trees sent forth golden oil, Christ is of two natures, two kinds of spirits dwell in the cosmos — good ones and evil ones, there are two great celestial lights, two equinoxes, two elements that beget the living spirit — earth and water...

And Mr Turk adds: There are two riverbanks one can stand on, two principal faiths one can profess, dual is the nature of the creature in Grandmother Davidovič's pantry, a birdlike one and a ratlike one, there are two Paskals, two mountaineers recruited by the Bartholomew knaves, and one day they will have two successors. There are two worlds — the pre-Olšany one and the Olšany one — and they are governed by two motions — by ascent and descent.

It would have been possible to go on elaborating the Olšany cabala for a long time had Mr Turk not suddenly remembered Mr Klečka — even they formed a twosome. At that moment Mr

Turk feels the autumnal chill penetrating his body, for how can one person warm himself alone? And as Mr Turk peeks out of the tomb over the shoulder of the melancholy angel (he may be looking to see if, by chance, Mr Klečka isn't returning with the autumn), he notices that the graveyard vineyard is dusted with white — hoarfrost.

THE CEMETERY SUBSTANCE

Diviš, who has eaten the Bartholomew almond, is trying mentally to justify himself: The almond is Christ, for the Saviour's divinity is like a kernel enclosed in a human shell. And if Mr Turk were to join him in his contemplation, he would say that the Hebrew word *luz* means both an almond tree and a subterranean city of immortals. But beware, Diviš — this is a Bartholomew city. Of course it is also true that one bitter almond is enough to poison a rat or a bat, or perhaps a cemetery squirrel.

That's just what Diviš is thinking about as he breaks the promise he made to Mr Turk. When one of the tame squirrels trustingly looks for a nut in his hand, Diviš wonders whether such a squirrel could be the reincarnation of a dead soul hoping to find the nut of immortality.

No, Diviš has no intention of disturbing Nanynka Shmid's sleep, Mr Turk's words are deeply etched in his memory, he wants to let Nanynka Shmid rest in peace (and yet the poor creature has woken up, she probably senses Diviš nearby). As Diviš walks through the cemetery, he begins to succumb to melancholy. He wonders whether his melancholy could be connected in any way with the time he scraped the skin off his fingers on the hardened cemetery soil. That day, his blood must have been invaded by the slowly but surely advancing infection, by the long illness that disintegrates the tissue of dreams and the web of hopes, weakens the will to act and infuses deadly inertia into the limbs and, above all, the mind.

Just as Diviš reaches this point in his graveyard meditation and is carefully examining his fingers, Bernard Bolzano addresses him — Paskal (aren't you a descendant of the famous Pascal?), have you read my *Athanasia, or Grounds for the Immortality of the Soul*? I am presently contemplating its new version. I have introduced into my system the concept of cemetery substance, eternal and indestructible, animated and endowed with imagination. This substance can be infinitely perfected but also — here Bernard Bolzano lowers his voice — infinitely corrupted. Just look around you, Paskal, all those leprous dreams engendered by this substance, and subsequently annihilated by it. And all around just words, words, words...

Diviš continues on his way, penetrating ever deeper into the cemetery space from where faint sounds of voices occasionally reach his ears. Suddenly Mr Erben cries out that he sees a mountain rising above all others. — Mr Erben is at his prophesying again, comments Grandmother Davidovič in the pantry. What mountain does he have in mind? If Horngoat or Hoardgold were saying that, they would definitely mean the Grossglockner. If it were Markéta Paskal, it undoubtedly would be Kutná Mountain that swallowed up Diviš's grandmother more than half a century before. And if it were Jan Tůňka, he would have Blaník Mountain, his mountain-abyss, before his eyes. But what sort of mountain can Mr Erben be seeing here at the cemetery, isn't he once again misleading himself and others with false hope? Then Diviš notices that the eye of the poet is contemplating a pile of rotting leaves heaped up near his grave. So that's his mountain! As a matter of fact, there is nothing strange in that, everybody simply has a mountain of his own, proportionate to the life allotted him. However, if everything is thus relative and transient, isn't it irrelevant whether or not Diviš eats an almond? Alice Davidovič probably wouldn't accept this kind of reasoning. Diviš's hesitancy and Diviš's readiness to come up with excuses for himself are profoundly alien to her. Of course, it is not all irrelevant, for if everything does repeat itself, then Diviš will have to swallow a bitter almond several more times (he should just take a look at

Mr Sabina, and he needn't even look so far — he should just take a look at his own father), and the offence, which up to now has seemed hazy, will loom in full clarity. If only things were as obvious to Diviš as they are to Alice. If only Diviš weren't feeling the deadly fatigue of body and soul as he tries to walk through the cemetery, barely able to drag his feet. Alice is helping him, she hasn't yet completely rejected Diviš, not yet. But what is Diviš to do when Bolzano's cemetery substance has penetrated all his pores, and also the scraped skin on his fingers?

— An intruder and a werewolf, that's what he is, says Grandmother Davidovič in the pantry. — Serves him right, he's been asking for it.

CONSOLIDATION AT OLŠANY

The consolidation process is under way. It is under way in the Spanish Hall, and also at Olšany. Vinohradská Avenue is being consolidated and Zásmuky Lane too. These little lanes, leading from nowhere to nowhere, are always suspicious and may harbour all sorts of dangers. The unsuspecting pedestrian passing through them might suddenly find himself confronted with a dismal view, as happened to Nanynka Shmid the other day while walking along with Diviš Paskal. She hid her head under his reindeer sweater, but even through the sweater she could see the lane leading to the cemetery, there was nowhere to hide from the sight — not even under Diviš's sweater, least of all under there, because by then Diviš himself was already half dead. That's why Nanynka could go with him in the first place, that's why she could expect something from him, but since Diviš was only half dead, she couldn't actually stay with him, that would have ended badly for both of them, as Mr Turk explained to her later on, and Mr Turk is a very wise man. Mr Turk has not always been like that, it was here at Olšany that he grew wise. He saw what others didn't see, heard what others didn't hear, for here at Olšany everything appears much more clearly defined, and he who wants to, he who dares, may begin to see. But there are many more of those who prefer to hide their heads in their little molehill graves and dig in their little graveyard gardens without looking left or right. And this is what the Olšany consolidation is all about: to make everyone just like that, with no interest in anything else. As a side effect of this continuous process, the post-mortal life (some life, contends Alice Davidovič, a vegetative condition at most, and even that is not the right term — a sepulchral condition) overflows its banks, gradually pouring over the cemetery wall and spilling into the adjoining streets and lanes. And what has been alive on the other side of the wall grows gradually numb and passes over the wall. That is a passage of the highest order — pascha — pesah. The dead seem to be coming to life and the living struggle along as if dead. And no one is able to tell where life ends and where death begins.

— All is vanity, nothing but vanity, says Mr Turk. One even grows accustomed to death and somehow doesn't seem to mind it. There are but few who won't resign themselves to it, and if one emptiness could hurt another emptiness, those would have stones cast at them by the others. So they get stoned at least with words, at least with those. One may be hit by a word in such a way that he never gets up again, another may lose his mind — like Mr Klečka who hands out flowers to everyone and nobody knows what it means.

No sooner does Mr Turk remember Mr Klečka (he now feels almost no pain at the memory, because it seems to him a long time since Mr Klečka left him), than he sees his friend coming over. Nanynka Shmid, the little virgin of Olšany, is leading him across the snow. Mr Klečka is smiling at Mr Turk as if nothing at all has happened, as if he has just been looking around awhile. Nanynka and Mr Klečka proceed to tell Mr Turk about Benjamin (the episode has become a legend to them by now), about how they brought Benjamin over from Hagibor, and how Benjamin dissolved before their eyes, and all that because of Mr Hamza.

— Oh no, Mr Turk shakes his head. — It was bound to happen

147

anyway. And if it hadn't been Mr Hamza, it would have been someone else. Maybe even me, or you. Nanynka and Mr Klečka look at Mr Turk in amazement. — You wouldn't even realize it. Every living thing passes away, and what is dead passes away doubly so. And a dream born here at Olšany, even though it may have materialized, vanishes more easily than anything else. Who has ever been sated by a little lamb never even conceived?

Finally they have to admit he is right, only Mr Klečka objects that the dream was a very beautiful one. As for Mr Turk, he was never able to dream, he could dream only the time he was feverish and wanted to pick a bunch of grapes at the cemetery, that's why he is worse off here than others. — Yet even here it is possible to experience something beautiful, says Mr Klečka, and Nanynka agrees.

So even they, thinks Mr Turk, even they have grown accustomed to this place, they have found a little garden of their own here. Perhaps it must be so if one wants to survive — survive what? But Mr Turk will not resign himself to it, not he. He and who else? Perhaps he should look for others who aren't resigned, but Mr Turk is already old and tired — from that sepulchral condition as Alice Davidovič would say, but above all from resisting the resignation, always so very exhausting, as well as from his graveyard wisdom, whose burden he must carry, never to be relieved by anyone, not even by death. Poor Mr Turk! Great Mr Turk!

THE LAST BALL

Horngoat and Hoardgold are chasing Doe all over Hagibor. Doe used to be the premier ball boy, nobody was as agile as he, but by now he is a little old man, catching him is easy. And the hunters don't even have to resort to a ruse, they don't have to slip a virgin's lap in the unicorn's path (didn't Doe at one time dream of Nora Pelt's lap?). Now they are taking Doe to Major Bartošek in Bartholomew Street.

— So you are Doe, Hagibor's premier ball boy, says Major Bartošek and Doe nods, still hardly able to catch his breath after the Hagibor chase. — Doe, who was it that you took in? In that moment Doe grows sad, remembering his lost son, his Benjamin. And then suddenly he begins to think — what if Benjamin is here and no mishap befell him, as he has feared. Doe softly pronounces Benjamin's name. Major Bartošek doesn't fail to notice that it is a Jewish name, straight out of the Old Testament, and thus he is even more interested. — And where has he gone, this Benjamin of yours? Doe doesn't know, he really doesn't know, Doe begs the gentlemen not to prolong the torture and to tell him if they have Benjamin, he has been so afraid that something bad has happened to him. — Doe, we're not interested in such stories here. That Benjamin of yours is a subversive element and you were hiding him. But his Benjamin was only picking up tennis balls as he himself once used to do....

— We know about that kind of ball boy, says Major Bartošek, while crunching an almond and offering two more to Horngoat and Hoardgold. — Today he's picking up tennis balls and to-morrow he'll come up with the idea of using them to set fire to a tank.... So that's what they have on Doe, that he was throwing tennis balls at the vehicles carrying the plague knaves? And on top of that they accuse Doe of trying to restore the First Republic. Doe hears a torrent of words, of Bartholomew words, none among them offering a glimmer of hope that he might find his Benjamin. He would throw a tennis ball at these, too, if only he had one. Doe feels about the floor around him but doesn't find a single ball to throw in their faces, they must have taken his tennis balls away back at Hagibor, he always used to have some on him, what Doe would give now for even a single ball.

The dark night of St Bartholomew's Day descends upon Jan Paskal, who is losing his sight and his hearing. Silkworm Paskal wraps the night around his body, placing his head in its dark lap. But suddenly, as if from nowhere, there appears an ugly old woman who says: Puscall, you're not a unicorn, you're just an ordinary cuckold. And Paskal would like to bury his head even deeper into the night, to hide there from that inexorable old woman, but it's impossible. For she is Grandmother Davidovič, herself emerging from the same night, and the deeper Paskal sinks his head into it, the closer Grandmother Davidovič comes to him, the more his throat constricts. Jan Paskal feels his neck but finds nothing — only a barely perceptible groove, as if his head were separating from his body. With every day, however, the little groove grows more and more distinct. It is the groove left behind by a clerical collar, by a Bartholomew collar.

— Shame on you, a priest and you couldn't even find the little head of Christ… I met that deaf-mute Anna of yours in Poland, we flew out of the chimney together. This is not the first time she has attacked Paskal in that way, lately, Grandmother Davidovič keeps coming out of the pantry more and more often. And Paskal keeps curling up into himself ever more tightly.

And when Diviš comes in and sees Grandmother Davidovič, and sees his father turning into a silkworm, he knows right away what has happened. — Grandmother, you'd better go and keep an eye on Grandfather Davidovič, so he doesn't run away from you to Mrs Soška again. Diviš's words work like magic, Grandmother Davidovič scurries off to the pantry at once, never even glancing at Paskal. But as soon as Diviš steps aside, Grandmother Davidovič is back in the room again.

— And what have you done with Kain, Puscall? He was just crazy about your mother. Grandmother Davidovič gives a sigh: Poor thing, what became of her in Kutná Mountain? Jan Paskal knows what went on: year after year his father travelled to see her and begged her to come back. Later on he would merely watch her from a distance and then leave again. At first she acted in the theatre, she couldn't live without it, and then even that came to an end and she turned to scrubbing the theatre steps. Back home Father would weep on Kain's shoulder. Then one day he decided to take his son along, but by then it was too late, the Mountain had carried her away. Naturally, Grandmother Davidovič knows all this and is just putting Paskal to the test, to see if she can't stir up his conscience or at least some feeling of remorse in him, from there it would just be an easy step…. Then Grandmother Davidovič would know how to handle him, just as she learned how to handle Grandfather. As long as Grandfather wouldn't try to leave again.

Grandmother hurries back into the pantry. And she sees: Grandfather Davidovič is just lowering his feet, about to get up from his bed. He gives a wry laugh at Grandmother's catching him in the act and settles back to sleep. Since what else is left for him but his pantry sleep, at least there Grandmother can't pursue him. And Grandmother, knowing only too well that Grandfather always gives her the slip this way, makes a point of telling him at length what's new outside, and Grandfather keeps listening because he's curious and can't sleep. — Would you look at him, look at Silkworm Paskal, he wants to shed his cocoon, says Grandfather Davidovič after hearing out Grandmother's long speech. — Just a bit longer and a little moth will fly out.

Diviš Paskal perceives things differently. He doesn't like his father's wrapping himself up. Only a body is left sitting here and the head is wandering who knows where, it detached itself from the trunk right where the clerical collar had left the little groove, that forbidden groove. From Diviš's point of view, Father's Bartholomewesque wrapping himself up into the night and into his conscience seems more like a wrapping for death than for a new life. And the unwrapping that will follow in due course, that Bartholomewesque unwrapping and shedding of skin, seems to Diviš even less connected with life. And to say that a moth will fly out! That's sheer mockery, since then he'll be dragging himself around the cemetery, with everyone shouting at him: Bartholomew Paskal — traitor of the nation! But which nation did he actually betray, there at the Little Bears, there in Bartholomew Street? Only himself. And yet they will all feel entitled to judge him, to sling mud at him, each and every one of them a handful in the name of the homeland. And when his wings grow heavy with the Olšany mud, and when in his muddy graveyard existence he'll be like them, only then will they be satisfied, although maybe not even quite then. Moreover it may still happen that the imperial eagle Hergesell will come to Olšany and strike him with his beak. In whose lap, in whose lap at Olšany will Paskal the unicorn, Puscall the cuckold, seek refuge?

THE POLABIAN SLAV
AND THE HARLOT OF OLŠANY

Herr Hergesell, who once studied *The Tibetan Book of the Dead*, belongs to the initiates, to those who upon finding themselves after death in the *bardo*, as this transitory state is called in Tibetan, are fully aware of the limits of their postmortal spiritual existence, they suffer its misery to the full and do not deceive themselves by any false hope of some favourable new reincarnation. Herr Hergesell knows that, should he be reincarnated, he would be but one of the unfortunate spirits called the *preta*. And, who knows, he might be reincarnated into an animal, perhaps a wolf, or a bird, perhaps an eagle, because his karma is unfavourable

— Come to my aid, help one wandering in the *bardo*, Herr Hergesell prays as he descends into the lightwell or glides above the Olšany Cemetery. And he doesn't know why it is, perhaps some past existence is awakening in him, that words from an ancient tongue now often surface in his memory, words in a tongue long since obliterated by German dialects. It is his maternal grandmother, who came from a town in Lusatia, who is speaking through him. And sometimes his grandmother appears to him in person, just as one of those strange Slavic words comes to his mind. And Herr Hergesell is afraid of his grandmother, even more so since he is not quite sure she isn't also Grandmother Davidovič from the pantry. And much as Herr Hergesell tries to convince himself that it's all just an illusion of the *bardo*, he is nevertheless filled with anxiety and would rather be reincarnated immediately in order to escape this, even if he were to exist only as a *preta*. And he searches for the gateway to a womb he might enter.

Mr Kollár catches the sound of the ancient Slavic tongue, snippets of the language in which the *bardo* wanderer thinks aloud every now and then, and he grows animated: — Are you a Polabian Slav? Herr Hergesell is amused by Mr Kollár's question, he cannot help laughing. It's a good thing that Alice Davidovič is nearby, she takes Mr Kollár by the hand, and quickly leads him away. She tries to explain to him who Herr Hergesell is, but Mr Kollár, the sweet Polabian idiom still sounding in his soul, shakes his head. Why, the language of that man is a pure Slavic language, once threatened by extinction, but behold, here it is born again, right here at Olšany, isn't that a miracle? — His grandmother was from Lusatia, Alice Davidovič says.

What could it be that allows Alice to see farther than others? Perhaps it is because Alice wants to see, because she doesn't close her eyes, doesn't passively give in to the general apathy, doesn't closet herself in her limited world but tries to enter other people's worlds, to lend others a helping hand, for Alice is convinced that even in such painful circumstances not all is lost, that there always remains some hope for the sake of which it is worth trying to suppress the deadly torpor, to stay awake as much as possible, not to succumb to the Olšany sleep. Whenever Alice feels sleep getting the better of her, she sets forth to a place where someone's fate is being decided, and joins in for a while. But how many like her are there around here? How many who strive to see beyond their muddy graves or their ornate marble headstones?

Herr Hergesell goes out of his way to avoid Alice, but she always appears from somewhere unexpected. She must have conspired with that grandmother from Lusatia. Herr Hergesell doesn't care for this Jewish girl, he'd like to get rid of her, but one emptiness cannot harm another, only through words can a wound be inflicted, only through words. But no sooner does he start thinking this way, than a grandmother suddenly appears before him — his grandmother from Lusatia or the grandmother from the pantry, or is it both of them in one person — shaking her finger at him. And without a word, Herr Hergesell leaves Alice alone. If only he could at last find the gateway to a womb through which he could pass and thus escape the phantoms from the *bardo*, whose number is constantly increasing, who are coming closer and closer, growing more and more aggressive. Even to become just an animal or a bird rather than being this emptiness, this ambiguous emptiness between life and death. And at this moment the wanderer in the *bardo* sees Nora Paskal.

Nora Paskal still has the mother-of-pearl button Pavel Santner so scornfully tossed away. As she turns the button to the various points of the compass, all kinds of images and events from her own life and from other people's lives appear before her eyes, for it is a button of remembrance. At one time she seems to see a Babylonian gazebo materializing in the middle of the cemetery, and at another, when she dares to flip the button, she is suddenly sitting astride Herr Hergesell's lap, as if she were riding an apocalyptic beast.

And sometimes this scene becomes so suggestive, not only for Nora but also for the other Olšany dwellers, that they begin to gather around her, pointing their fingers at her: The harlot of Olšany! And they want to expel her from their Olšany paradise. But she just mounts the back of Hergesell the wolf and manages to escape from them, for the inhabitants of Olšany are slow and tire easily.

Once again, Nora flips the button infernal side up. Already the imperial eagle Hergesell is swooping down towards her. No sooner do the eagle's wings hit the ground, than he changes into a dashing court clerk.

— Do you also find everything here so disgusting, Frau Lamm? Herr Hergesell kisses Nora Paskal's hand, although it is the same one with which she cut his throat. And a murmur runs through the cemetery: One has to admit those Germans do have good manners. But when Herr Hergesell puts Nora on his lap, another murmur runs through the cemetery, this one of indignation and outrage.

Once again, Nora mounts the apocalyptic beast, and their flight is wild. And when they alight upon the earth, they both feel very tired and lonelier than before. And they both feel an urge to hurt the other. — What is it like to make love to a saint? Herr Hergesell asks Nora. — What is it like to cuckold a saint?

Nora knows that a mere flip of the button would cut off the shameless wolf talk. No, she never supposed the wolf to be a lamb, not even when she was seating herself on his wolf lap, especially not then. And just as Nora Paskal seizes Herr Hergesell's neck in the naïve hope that a dead person can be killed again, a new life stirs within her — a lamb's life or a wolf's life, who can now tell one from the other, a life straddling two extremes, a life in both kinds. The more the new Diviš grows in Nora, the weaker the first Diviš will become, feeling increasingly torn between the house and the cemetery.

Nora is strangling Hergesell the eagle because she has no knife handy as she did then, thinking it possible to annihilate a sin within oneself and to redeem a lamb's skin with a wolf's blood. And when the others see that the imperial eagle Hergesell is at his last gasp, though it is only illusory and temporary, they begin to contemplate a revolution. But Nora quickly flips the button because she's had enough of all those revolutions, and they humbly disperse and return to their graves. Yet as they are leaving, they can't resist flinging some Olšany mud at the harlot, each his own handful in the name of the homeland, each his own Olšany handful.

Behold Georgie Briar, clad in a mouse-grey overcoat, marching all by himself to Bubeník's pub. There, at the counter whose shiny surface reflects his new look, Georgie drinks his living water. And everyone is astonished: How come Georgie, who has been cursed into the form of an eternal child for all these years, is now having a drink here all by himself? Perhaps it's the overcoat that did it, the overcoat Caretaker Briar used to wear when he went to stoke the furnace. One day the smoke made him faint, he fell down and suffocated. Maybe anyone who puts on that overcoat is suddenly grown up and assumes the now vacant place. For things contain a strange fluid called aura, and whoever comes into contact with the aura will grow to resemble its former owner and suffer a similar fate.

The process of Georgie's individuation is nearing its end. It culminates right there at the counter where Georgie examines his new look with delight. And then he goes back to watching over the house through the little window onto the hallway and to stoking the furnace. The expedition into the lightwell has long been forgotten, that happened during the dark reign of the kingdom of the sofa. When Diviš Paskal passes by, a dim bitter memory of a stolen fleece crosses the mind of the one in the mouse-grey overcoat. And he thinks: People of his sort shouldn't be trusted. And the eyes of Briar II carefully follow Diviš Paskal until he disappears around the bend in the hallway. The one in the mouse-grey overcoat is aware of his own power, now he no longer needs to stab with a pin, not any more. He knows he can just point his finger and someone's fate will be decided. And should Alice Davidovič beg for mercy now, he will be pitiless, a muff means nothing to this Georgie, not even one of Persian lamb. But Alice won't come looking for the successor, Alice is not one to beg for mercy, definitely not twice, and certainly not from those in mouse-grey overcoats.

And Mr Turk, who is relating parables at the cemetery, speaks of the reign of Jupiter, which succeeded the reign of Saturn. And who knows if here there wasn't also a stone, a chunk of coal or coke on which the caretaker choked to death, who knows? But as parables are fulfilled anew, they also undergo changes in a way that makes one pass into another or melds several parables into one. Thus the parable of Jupiter-Georgie is at the same time the parable of the Minotaur (after all, stuck somewhere in his story there is also a pin), an animal to whom the house must deliver a sacrificial lamb each year, an Olšany lamb, so that its inhabitants can live in peace for another year. And maybe he would be satisfied with a lamb or at least with someone bearing a lamb-like name. In his conceit, however, the one with a lamb-like name believes himself to be a new Theseus, and Alice to him is Ariadne, who will lead him out of the briary labyrinth. Mr Turk gravely shakes his head: His arrogance will prove fatal to him, and that in no time.

HELIOTROPISM

More and more frequently Jan Paskal recalls his childhood, his childhood in Kain's shadow. The closer he comes to death, the more he recalls his childhood. He's not afraid of it, for death crept up on him already years ago in the form of the two Bartholomew knaves, once a week death dined with him at the Little Bears. Should death resemble either of those two — Horngoat or Hoardgold — he would follow it quite meekly and not even put up a fight, by now he knows the story of their mountain ascents and descents by heart. This kind of death, this flaying, ceased to upset him long ago, it had become a habit. Actually, Jan Paskal no longer even feels embarrassed standing before them in his Bartholomew nakedness, his skin flung over his arm like a cloak. But of late things are not as they were before. More and more frequently, the talk at the Little Bears keeps turning to some other two men — Randy and Slash. For the time of the changing of the guard in Bartholomew Street has come. Those coming in are much more rapacious, much more self-confident, much more ambitious, to them Jan Paskal is just a useless screw-loose old man, while Horngoat and Hoardgold are clowns who must be removed.

At the Little Bears, Randy and Slash join their table and order a Bastion of Tábor. And while they lay siege to the bastion on their plates, Horngoat and Hoardgold are climbing a mountain again, but it's no longer the Grossglockner, now they prefer to call it Salavat-dag, they have just reached its peak and from up there they look down at Randy and Slash. Down below Randy and Slash are making faces (meanwhile the Bastion of Tábor has fallen and lies at their feet), and Horngoat and Hoardgold sense that the other two don't trust them, or that a climb of this sort means nothing to them. That must be it. Members of their generation have some altogether different climbs under their belts, some altogether different memories, if any at all, since they consider reminiscing to be effeminate. Jan Paskal alone nods his head in appreciation, even he for a brief moment was at the summit with those two men. — Why climb when you can drive all the way up, says Randy. — And then, it wasn't really Salavat-dag but the Grossglockner, says Slash.

Horngoat and Hoardgold fall silent, after all what can they say since an abyss has opened up below them, and awaiting them at the bottom are not Anemone's open arms but those two men. And perhaps because Jan Paskal, in his imagination, has climbed so high in the mountains, where the air is thin, he suddenly has difficulty breathing, something seizes his throat from both sides. Precisely this is what he has feared, that death would come for him in the form of wood brought to life, permeated with a peculiar scent. Precisely now has Jan Paskal become aware of this and knows that if he turned around, he would find Kain standing behind him, wooden Kain who has come for supper at the Little Bears, as though the fire in the small Budějovice courtyard had never even touched him.

— Those two will also have their turn one day, says Mr Turk, meaning Randy and Slash. One day two others will appear and laugh at them for a change. Bartholomew grass lasts as long as it lasts. And that's exactly what Grandmother Davidovič in the pantry has been thinking, she often finds herself in agreement with Mr Turk, and no wonder, they share the same ancient wisdom after all, and similar life experience.

What is referred to as heliotropism in the world of plants, namely the phenomenon of plants turning in the direction of the strongest source of light and trying to adopt an advantageous position in relation to that light source, Mr Turk, in the world of humans, refers to as turnsoulism. This manifests itself outwardly in acts of curving, bending and expanding (before devoting himself to the study of silkworms, Mr Turk once wrote a paper on heliotropism). Thus the Huguenot, Jean de Pascal, during the St Bartholomew's Day Massacre, attaches a white rag to one of his sleeves to look like a papist, and saves his neck. His flight to Bohemia is then simply a flight from his own betrayal. And later on his descendant Jan Paskal, who invented this Huguenot tale, albeit somewhat differently, for reasons of carnal sin converts to the Protestant faith and to communion in both kinds. And so it is quite natural that upon his arrival at the Olšany Cemetery, Mr Klečka hands Jan Paskal a fuzzy turnsole leaf.

Jan Paskal is not yet familiar with Mr Klečka's flower symbolism and stands perplexed, the leaf in his hand, on a remote path in the cemetery. — So you're here now too, Thomas Hamza says to him by way of welcome. — You should tuck that leaf safely away, take my advice, nobody knows if it's not a sign of election, one day those who present it might even be reborn. Goatish heresies, thinks Jan Paskal. He finds it strange, however, that Mr Hamza of all people, he who always had a rational mind and stayed away from any kind of mysticism, falls for such ideas. Life in these conditions probably changes people a great deal. And though Jan Paskal has his doubts, he keeps the leaf, not daring to throw it away. And since the little groove left on his neck by his clerical collar has become very conspicuous these days, he holds the leaf so as to cover the groove.

Caretaker Briar is already pointing his finger at him: Look at that, why is he covering his neck with that leaf! What if he's a leper?! In a split second the turnsole leaf is torn away and the fatal groove of his conversion appears before everyone's eyes. And to erase the suspicion that the groove was made by a noose, Jan Paskal must tell his life story in the Olšany purgatory. When he finishes, he feels very tired and rather depressed and collapses into the graveyard grass. He is almost asleep when Nanynka Shmid approaches him: How is your Diviš, will he soon...? Jan Paskal is falling asleep in the lap of a virgin, Paskal the cuckold is sleeping in the place where earlier lay the traitor of the nation's hat. And Nanynka doesn't mind, to her they are all just very unhappy and weak creatures in need of comfort. Besides, this one is Diviš's father and soon ... soon Diviš will be.... So what could be wrong with this?

RELICS AND SYMBOLS

Souls cling to life through things, or rather through the relics of things. As if these relics hold some kind of promise of being reborn, the pledge of a new life. There is, after all, the aura, that extraordinary fluid surrounding and animating things, which the dead perceive much more strongly than the living. To touch things is almost like touching life itself.

Behold Thomas Hamza's handkerchief, torn in two. Behold the button Pavel Santner found and threw away, and which Nora Paskal is holding still, turning it and reminiscing. Behold Grandmother Davidovič's Sabbath tablecloth and her Persian lamb muff, which underwent several metamorphoses into a Persian lamb. For a thing in the world of the dead can for a time cease to be a thing and become instead an image, a symbol, a mere word. All these metamorphoses of things into images and of images into things are, however, only temporary, and soon things fall back into their ordinary, purely practical interrelations. All that then remains of the image and the form is merely a longing, a very strange longing.

Within things, however, there also lies hidden the threat of destruction, for they are snares and pitfalls awaiting the souls. He who gets caught in the snare of a thing, be it a scrap of cloth or a button, has indeed touched life for a moment, but the longing that subsequently overcomes him fills a much larger interval. And then — there is the unfortunate tension between the two worlds that afflicts possessors of relics. Thou shalt not take things belonging to the living — sounds one Olšany commandment.

— They are much too conceited, these hybrids, says Mr Köck, who also has been dwelling in the eternity of Olšany for some time now. — They're trying to raise themselves above us ordinary mortals by pretending that they're different, that they're less dead. Anybody could do that, but how would it look? Mr Köck is a staunch supporter of unity at Olšany, and to him the hybrids are no less traitors than, say, Mr Sabina. And there are more like Mr Köck around, even Caretaker Briar is on his side, he has already pointed his finger at many a hybrid (he has pointed at Mr Turk and at Alice Davidovič, too — Caretaker Briar can't stand Jews even here). And Thomas Hamza, who has long been biding his time, also joins in, by now he has become wiser, now he wouldn't struggle any more over a scrap of cloth with Nanynka Shmid, not any more. By the way, even Nanynka Shmid is suspect, she held in her lap the traitor of the nation's hat and walked about with the torn handkerchief, and then — she is so strangely wan. And God knows how things stand with Mr Klečka who has lost his mind, that is if he's not just pretending to have lost it.

— Who knows what's behind Mr Klečka's floral gifts, maybe they conceal some secret political symbolism, maybe they're signals the conspirators use to communicate with each other, says Mr Köck and ruthlessly crushes into the ground the corncockle he got from Mr Klečka. Thomas Hamza fully agrees with his action but doesn't admit to Mr Köck that just to play it safe he has carefully saved and dried the burdock leaf Mr Klečka gave him. From time to time Thomas Hamza secretly examines the leaf to see whether any images, any faces, have begun to appear on it.

But how to explain that Caretaker Briar never got any graveyard flower or a leaf from Mr Klečka? Instead, whenever Mr Klečka passes Briar, he begins to clutch his belly in a ridiculous way, sticking it out as if he were pregnant. Some might think that Mr Klečka has lost his mind because of the strange manner in which he lived his life, but Caretaker Briar knows that Mr Klečka is mimicking the way he used to carry food under his loden coat to Mr Turk at the cemetery during the war, and that he is also imitating Caretaker Briar who hid Alice Davidovič's muff under his coat. And from this pantomime Caretaker Briar concludes that Mr Klečka is probably not quite as crazy as he pretends to be. And Caretaker Briar even tries to tell Alice Davidovič that Mr Klečka is making fun of her delicate condition. Alice Davidovič doesn't quite believe this, especially coming from Caretaker Briar, but she seeks out Mr Klečka anyway. And when Mr Klečka sees Alice Davidovič, he hands her a pink motherwort: Because you're expecting Pavel Santner's baby. Such a handsome young man, says Mr Klečka — Poor Mr Turk, he thinks I'll bring him bread, but how can I bring it to him when I'm alive and he's dead?

And Alice Davidovič suddenly understands how things are with Mr Klečka. So Mr Klečka thinks that he's still alive, a strange kind of craziness, indeed. Alice thanks Mr Klečka for the motherwort and slips the flower into her hair. Why did she, even for a moment, believe Caretaker Briar's evil words? As if she didn't know him! And Alice Davidovič heads toward the gate because she feels cramped in the cemetery.

Diviš Paskal is standing at the gate. He gives Alice a long look, rather like when he returned from the lightwell and saw her down in the street for the first time. Alice Davidovič of course knows that a while ago wooden Kain came to fetch Diviš's father at the Little Bears and carried him off on his back, just as Paskal had once done with Kain. And in the pantry Grandmother and

Grandfather are probably very happy that there is one less person in the flat now and soon the flat will be entirely theirs. And suddenly, without knowing why, Alice feels sorry for Diviš and gives him the motherwort from her hair. The motherwort in the meantime has withered, and as Diviš takes it between two fingers, touching it but very lightly, it turns to dust. For nothing whole can pass from the dead to the living, only fragments of words, of ideas, and of images.

When Grandmother Davidovič sees them, she throws up her arms. — The last thing I ever expected in life was you two walking in together. But she doesn't mean it badly, she must have forgiven Diviš by now, since Diviš is almost one of their own. And Diviš notices that the bird sleeping near the ceiling has just awakened from its pantry sleep and has cheerfully flapped its wings — a hybrid bird, half bird and half rat, who has been dwelling here since the time of Diviš's childhood. And this is yet another prefiguration, yet another prophecy whose meaning just now is beginning to emerge. Behold Diviš taut between two beings, Diviš the hybrid, Dionysus-Diviš. And should Diviš one day be torn to pieces, thus fulfilling the myth connected with his name, it will be accomplished through words he has uttered and through images he himself has evoked — Dionysus Zagreus — Diviš the Lacerated.

DEATH OF THE BURYING BEETLE

O, Olšany, a chosen place!

The burying beetle is sacred at Olšany, it is virtually a totemic beetle whom the souls of the Olšany tribe may not touch. Woe to him who crushes it — as did Jan Paskal. Someone may only have accused him of murdering the insect, possibly Caretaker Briar, it might not have been Jan Paskal at all who dispatched the burying beetle from the world, yet once the accusation stuck to him, it was impossible to be rid of it. And when after the crime the delinquent is approached by the two Olšany knaves — Horngoat and Hoardgold (so they're here too now, that happened fast), Jan Paskal is already quite compliant. All they want from him is to note what kind of ideas Mr Turk or Mr Havlíček are spreading, and then, in a remote corner, to have a chat with them about that. And they in turn promise to keep quiet about the dead beetle. And about Diviš's paternal descent, too.

Jan Paskal doesn't quite understand the connection between the burying beetle and Diviš. Perhaps they mention Diviš in connection with the little beetle because he had crushed him too, being uncertain of his paternity. For years he kept finding in Diviš, by turns, his own traits and traits of the other one, as if Diviš could have been the son of two fathers, as if Diviš had a dual nature. Yet what if these two men possess some truly irrefutable evidence? Can't their evidence, however, be just as false and fabricated as the dead burying beetle about which Mr Turk states with certainty (and Mr Turk knows because he was an entomologist) that it was not in fact a burying beetle? But in the end who is to be believed? One can't even believe Nanynka Shmid, although she is still a child, not even her.

Jan Paskal tries to stand up but suddenly sees Nora Pelt approaching, she is Miss Pelt to him again, as before their marriage. He would like to believe her but how can he after all that has happened? — After all what has happened? asks Nora Pelt. And Jan Paskal knows that Nora is right, because it was Jan Paskal himself who led her to him, back then when he gave him the Eucharist. And maybe even earlier. And she then purposely leaves him to his doubts because she scorns him for his weak and irresolute character. He couldn't bring himself to slit the wolf's throat. — You couldn't even kill the burying beetle, not even that, she hurls at his face. Jan Paskal sinks into the grass. It's a good thing one is at least allowed to sleep here, to sleep a lot, nobody is against one sleeping. Only to sleep and not to see and not to hear. But what if the dreams we will dream won't be much better, or more comforting? And what if life, or rather death, is nothing but a dream, an ugly Olšany nightmare that frightens us towards morning?

O, Olšany, plague-stricken city!

THE BARTHOLOMEW BROOD

In a little garden of delight, in a little Bartholomew garden, Diviš
is embracing white Claudia. Some kind of wheel is turning there,
Diviš takes it for a windmill because that is easier than admitting
it's something else, more bearable than going to take a closer look
at that mill of his and seeing that someone's body is fastened to
it. When Diviš embraces white Claudia, he immediately forgets
about Alice, whom he wanted to take from the pantry, and even
about Nanynka Shmid, whom he wanted to take from the cemetery. After all, they are both dead, and how can one embrace a
dead girl, let alone marry her? Yet wasn't Diviš saying something
different before?

Alice would like to be objective, but it is so difficult to watch
Diviš embracing that live Bartholomew virgin. Some virgin! —
Bartošek's whore! A new life is already growing in her womb. A
lamb or a wolf cub — Paskal's or Bartošek's child, who knows,
Alice won't tell Diviš, let him suffer the anguish of uncertainty
since he has chosen a Bartholomew harlot over a … Over a dead
spinster. Alice has always feared Diviš might say that one day.
She has been longing to hear him say something utterly different,
waiting for the miraculous word by which he would take her away,
out of the Olšany emptiness, a word through which her soul would
be reincarnated once more into a human being, because, despite
everything she has been saying and thinking, this is what she has
been secretly wishing, on what she has set her heart. But Diviš
is no saviour, as he has pretended in his arrogance, and it was
naïve of Alice to think he might be the one to make this happen.

The pantry of late has become an even more sorrowful place
than before. — That Bartholomew brood, they multiply like
mushrooms after the rain, says Grandfather Davidovič. — See,
and you thought we'd be here alone again. Grandfather Davidovič

is right but Grandmother Davidovič won't admit it. She's wondering about Alice, where she might be. Ever since Alice rushed out of the window to meet Pavel Santner, Grandmother Davidovič can't shake off the feeling that something bad is happening to her.

DOWN THERE

Diviš is forever preparing to ask Alice a question: How does it feel to be falling, to find oneself between heaven and earth? But he never does put the question to Alice, and she, though well aware of what is on Diviš's mind, wouldn't answer it. After all, what is she supposed to tell him, how at that moment she felt Pavel Santner embracing her with such force that it hurt, and Benjamin, the youngest of the Davidovič line, was conceived in her? Her head went spinning and she dropped the muff she had taken along for the trip, for it was wintertime and snow was falling, although the snow was melting so fast that it turned into water as soon as it touched the ground.

And only then, in the grey slush, did Alice realize it hadn't been Pavel Santner but a whirlpool of air that had formed under her falling body. And when down there she looked around, and instead of her sweetheart saw Caretaker Briar bending over her, she knew right then she had made a mistake. She tried to reach for the muff and cover her bloodied face with it, but she couldn't move her hand, she couldn't even manage to turn her head in the direction of Caretaker Briar, who was walking away with the muff hidden under his grey overcoat. No, she should not have let go of the muff, she should not have opened her arms so wide to the one she was going to meet, she knew then for certain that she had been naïve, she knew it then. And the feeling one has while leaving one's body, while abandoning it the way a snake abandons its shed skin, then the brief feeling of relief at being free of pain — there is no way she can share that with Diviš. There is even a bit of nostalgia in it, as if the soul were beginning to suspect that it can never separate from the body completely, that a tormenting memory will linger forever, some vague notion, some hazy hope.

Alice slowly slips out of Diviš's arms: Stop fooling yourself, Diviš. What we're feeling for each other is not love, it's an altogether different feeling. — But what is it if it's not love, what feeling is it? Alice, however, doesn't answer Diviš, Alice is no longer sitting next to him.

I wish I were an angel made of stone, sighs Alice Davidovič as she passes the tomb inhabited by Mr Turk, such an angel has neither memories nor hopes, he evanesces and disintegrates. Stone is dead.

The melancholy angel softly smiles at Alice's naïveté. So he only evanesces and disintegrates? And stone is completely dead? If only Alice knew how everything within him is working toward a transformation, how he is awakening, slowly, alas, very slowly. But the day will come, maybe it's already near, when all graveyard angels dreaming their petrified graveyard dreams will step down from their tombstones and leave the plague-infested vineyard. And that very same day all dressmaker dummies will also come to life. One day...

THE MELANCHOLY ANGEL

I am the melancholy angel, certainly not Dürer's angel — I am an angel made by the master stonecutter from near the Olšany pond. Only the gesture of an arm supporting an overly heavy head is reminiscent of Dürer's angel, and no longer even that one, because one day in May the arm ceased to support the head and fell off. And my face, my melancholy face is tilted, it's leaning low over an abyss, oh, who is going to support it now? It will be Mr Turk or Mr Klečka, or perhaps Nanynka Shmid. One of them will place the lost arm against the body, the arm will promptly grow back, once more it will become a support and the head will rest on it with relief. But it mustn't be done by Diviš Paskal the dissembler, one touch of his hand and all hope of renewed wholeness will be lost, the cleft between the trunk and the fallen limb will deepen, the head will grow heavier, will incline even lower.

I am the melancholy angel, overcome by fatigue, and the abyss at my feet, the promise of rest, hardly frightens me any more. It grows into me through tendrils of Olšany grass, covers me with greenish Olšany moss, washes me with lavish Olšany rains.

Now I am lying down. Water washes melancholy from my face, my head is again a mere stone searching for a place to rest somewhere farther down, as far down as possible. My dream of resurrection is suddenly very remote, did I ever really dream it? Was I ever really an angel, I, the melancholy stone? How blessed I now feel in my petrified inertia and insensitivity at the bottom of the abyss into which I have rolled as into a cosy den whose shape is precisely mine.

I am a stone and a vague notion is being born in me: one day the master stonecutter from the Olšany pond will lift me again from this comforting spot, will wrench me from my namelessness and shapelessness and carve the features of his own melancholy into me. For this is how everything is repeated and transformed. I already feel as if, once more, I am ceasing to be a stone. If only there were not this anxiety, this bitter grief settling on my face, making my head heavier and heavier. If only it weren't for the nostalgic longing for human life, which is cursed into some place between the stone and the pit, the fleeting moment in which animated matter is suspended over the edge of the abyss.

I am the melancholy angel. For how much longer?

A NEW CONCEPTION

Grandmother Davidovič is a prophetess, she knows everything, she knew it long before it happened, before Benjamin was born, before Hergesell the eagle carried him away and abandoned him at Hagibor. She even knew about Benjamin leaving Hagibor and setting out for the cemetery. She just didn't foresee that it would all end so quickly and that Hamza the tobacconist would be tangled up in it. She still can't make sense of it.

— That's what happens when someone gets involved with the dead, Grandmother Davidovič says. — Just remember how rashly Mr Hamza gave his handkerchief to Mrs Havlíček on the very day those plague knaves came here. And from then on he went downhill. But who knows if it wasn't rather the other way around, that he gave her the handkerchief because his own days were already numbered, since otherwise he wouldn't have paid any attention to her. Only later he realized he had made a mistake, and he thought everything would be fixed if he got the handkerchief back, but that just made it worse. Such a decent man, and then this…

Grandfather Davidovič in his corner gives a wry laugh. He tends to think it served Hamza right. Anyhow, Grandmother is making excuses for him only because he used to court her in her younger days. You mean Grandmother doesn't remember what happened with her muff? He coolly denied it, although he recognized it. Grandfather Davidovič knows such decent people, he knows them very well, they are the worst, because nobody sees through them in time. And the leprosy that's on the rise comes directly from them, from all those Hamzas and Paskals, from those wolves in sheep's clothing. When it comes down to it he almost prefers Caretaker Briar, one knows right away where one stands with him. Or even someone like Hergesell — Grandmother Davidovič covers Grandfather's mouth. Why must he always tempt him unnecessarily? As if their position weren't bad enough. And it's never so bad as not to get…

— Grandmother, Grandfather, Alice calls out from the pantry's threshold, looking all transformed. — Hasn't Pavel Santner been by? What on earth has possessed Alice again, just when Grandmother thought she had finally got over her love beyond the grave. Wasn't all that had happened enough already? And why is she so out of breath?

— I can feel him in me again. — Whom, dearie? — Benjamin, of course. And Alice runs off and Grandmother Davidovič knows that Alice is again rushing to meet Pavel Santner. So long as Alice hasn't lost her mind like Mr Klečka, thinks Grandfather Davidovič. But Grandmother Davidovič, as if having heard what Grandfather was thinking, shakes her head.

— Of course she hasn't gone mad. This is exactly the way it must be, everything round and round again. As long as it's not Ixion's wheel, crosses Grandfather Davidovič's mind. He isn't sure if this should gladden or grieve him. He finds no comfort in it. Grandfather Davidovič simply doesn't like wheels because he has terrible memories of one of them.

THE WINDOW OF THE CHILDREN'S ROOM

Claudia the white lady is wandering through the Olšany flat, she can't sleep. Now, after the birth of her child, everything is upside down — she sleeps during the day, stays awake at night. Watch your step, Claudia, Diviš would like to call out to her, as if Claudia were walking atop the ramparts of Vertebra, the city of rocks. — If you don't turn back, you'll perish, said Claudia to Diviš in Bartholomew Street. Yet hadn't he turned back long ago? But they each probably had a different turning back in mind, Claudia the Bartholomew one and he the Olšany one.

Diviš is slowly putting on the suit he wears to go to the theatre, as if he were not getting ready to leave for the boiler room of the power plant in Prague's suburb of Holešovice where he works, but for a predawn matinée. The collar of his white shirt has wrinkled a little and here and there some white threads cling to the suit. Diviš goes to the pantry to get a brush. The bird, Chamberlain, lightly grazes Diviš's face with his wing and the rat, Chambermaid, lightly grazes his leg with her back. The two old folks are sitting in the dark, silent, their hands folded in their laps. They obviously want to let Diviš know they're angry with him. Maybe they're sulking because he has brought Claudia home and because the flat resounds with a baby's crying. They probably think he has forgotten Alice because of those two. He hasn't, how could Diviš forget her? Ever since he first saw Alice standing down in the street, her gaze fixed on his window, she has always been somewhere nearby, always ready to interfere with his thoughts, to argue with Diviš about something, because she sees everything differently, inevitably so, since he is here and she there. Yesterday she told him: You should finally make up your mind, Diviš. Don't you realize it's impossible to live like this, in both kinds?

Grandmother Davidovič, watching Diviš carefully brush off his suit, says: I think our Alice is waiting in front of the house. And she looks at Diviš. And Diviš no longer thinks they're angry with him, they're just not being their usual selves, but somehow solemnly earnest. And Diviš senses this has something to do with him and with Alice. He goes to look out of the window of the children's room to see if Alice is standing down there. And indeed she is. It really is high time for Diviš to make up his mind, one way or the other. Whenever he tried to get from one side to the other — in the lightwell or in the pass — he stuck fast somewhere in the middle, ever since then he has been stuck there, unable to move either forward or backward. But here Diviš is just making excuses for himself, maybe he's simply not trying hard enough, maybe he doesn't really want this. For Alice to talk when she is down there is easy, up here everything is much more complicated, much more ambiguous. And isn't she herself really somewhere in the middle too, belonging neither quite here, nor there?

In this Alice Davidovič concedes that Diviš Paskal is right, she really is neither quite here nor there, that's where her trouble lies, but also her hope. It must be precisely this that brings them together, their being in the middle, although they come from opposite sides. And now they advance one towards the other, to give each other support.

December 1977–October 1978, June 1984

TRANSLATOR'S NOTE

While Daniela Hodrová's first novel *Podobojí* was quickly translated and published in several European languages after its original appearance in Czech, this English version has had a more arduous birth. My mother, Tatiana Firkusny, brought home the first edition of *Podobojí* from a trip to Prague in 1991. Drawn in by Hodrová's use of language, the novel's multiple layers of meaning, as well as its rich literary, historical and classical allusions, she was immediately captivated. It was she who announced: 'We must translate this into English. It's extraordinary.' And so, with Hodrová's blessing, we began. The first version of our translation, titled *In Both Species*, was completed in 1992. We sent the manuscript to several publishers, and subsequently also translated excerpts from the novels *Théta* and *Perunův den* (Perun's Day). The latter excerpts were published in the anthologies *Allskin and Other Tales by Contemporary Czech Women*, and *Daylight in Nightclub Inferno: Czech Fiction from the Post-Kundera Generation*, respectively, while an excerpt from *In Both Species* appeared in the literary journal *Prairie Schooner*. On the basis of that published excerpt in English, Hodrová won the 1992 Virginia Faulkner Award for Excellence in Writing. The complete translation of *Podobojí*, however, did not find a publisher.

In 2005, the year my mother died, our translation still languished unpublished. Five years later I re-discovered our manuscript, in its obsolete word-processed format, and decided to revise it. With Hodrová's continued blessing, version two of the translation, now with the working title *The Kingdom of Olšany*, made the rounds of several more publishers, but again to no avail. Then in spring of 2011, I received a phone message that an Elena Sokol had called, and would I please ring her back. It turned out Elena was calling on behalf of Hodrová, whose acquaintance she first made in Prague in 1996, through an interview for a project on contemporary Czech women writers. Already then, Hodrová had mentioned to Elena the existence of our unpublished translation of *Podobojí*, but our paths were destined to cross only much later. When in 2011 an American publisher approached Hodrová with an interest in commissioning a translation of *Podobojí*, unaware that a manuscript translation already existed, she decided to contact me. Having mislaid my coordinates, however, she turned to Elena for help. When we finally connected, Elena asked if she might read our translation, so I sent her the manuscript, inviting her to make comments. Soon I received the manuscript back, accompanied by a lovely postcard depicting Prague's Old Town Square in 1820, with a note, saying: 'I truly enjoyed reading the incredible translation of *Podobojí* that you and your mother created together. I hope my pencil marks will make more sense when I send you more general comments.... I look forward to our continued "conversation". And so, together, we undertook to revise the translation once again.

In conclusion, there are many acknowledgments without which this note would be incomplete. They begin with thanks to Daniela Hodrová, for her unwavering support of this translation; to Elena Sokol, thanks to whose loving and expert attention the original English translation was burnished into the richly nuanced and more poetic final version presented here; to my daughter Silvia Callegari, for re-typing the 1992 version into an editable document; to my family for patience and encouragement; to wonderfully supportive friends and colleagues who were willing and attentive first readers; to Jack Coling, our editor at Jantar Publishing, for his excellent suggestions; and finally to the late

Peter Kussi, who inspired my first attempts at translation, and to my mother, Tatiana Firkusny, who introduced me to Daniela Hodrová's world, and without whom this translation would not have come into being. In my heart, this work is dedicated to her.

Véronique Firkusny
New York City
August 2014

Also available from Jantar Publishing

PRAGUE. I SEE A CITY...
by Daniela Hodrová

Translation by David Short
Foreword by Rajendra Chitnis

Originally commissioned for a French series of alternative
guidebooks, Hodrová's novel is a conscious addition
to the tradition of Prague literary texts by, for example,
Karel Hynek Mácha, Jakub Arbes, Gustav Meyrink and
Franz Kafka, who present the city as a hostile living
creature or labyrinthine place of magic and mystery in
which the individual human being may easily get lost.

KYTICE
CZECH & ENGLISH BILINGUAL EDITION
by Karel Jaromír Erben

Translation and Introduction by Susan Reynolds

Kytice was inspired by Erben's love of Slavonic myth and
the folklore surrounding such creatures as the Noonday
Witch and the Water Goblin. First published in 1853,
these poems, along with Mácha's *Máj* and Němcová's
Babička, are the best loved and most widely read 19th
century Czech classics. Published in the expanded 1861
version, the collection has moved generations of artists
and composers, including Dvořák, Smetana and Janáček.

www.jantarpublishing.com

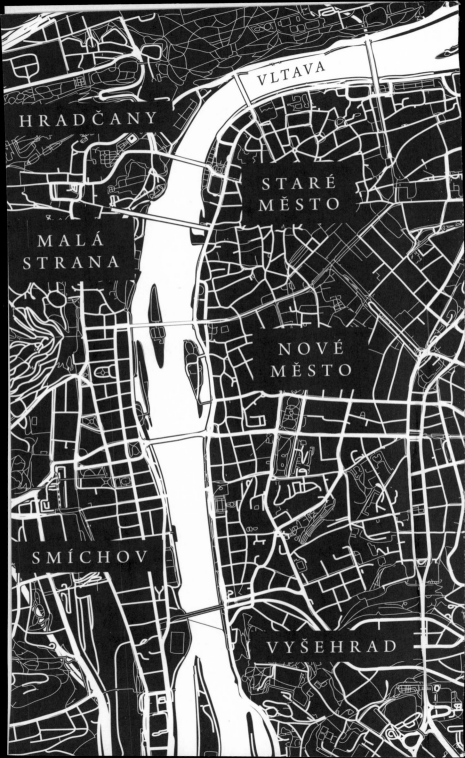